FOCUS ON THE FAMILY

A Man Called NORMAN

MIKE ADKINS

Tyndale House Publishers, Wheaton, Illinois

A MAN CALLED NORMAN

Copyright © 1989 by Focus on the Family

Library of Congress Cataloging-in-Publication Data
Adkins, Mike, 1942–
    A man called Norman / by Mike Adkins.
       p.   cm.
    ISBN 1-56179-714-6
    1. Corbin, Norman. 2. Adkins, Mike. 1942–
—Friends and associates. 3. Christian biography—United
States I. Title.
BR1725.C685A65 1989
209′.2′2—dc20   89-38596
[B]   CIP

A Focus on the Family Book published by
Tyndale House Publishers, Wheaton, Illinois 60189

Unless noted otherwise, all Scripture quotations are from
the King James Version.

Editor: Larry K. Weeden
Designer: Timothy Jones
Cover Illustration: Ron DiCianni

Printed in the United States of America

99 00 01 02 03 04 / 10 9 8 7 6 5 4

Acknowledgments

Several people gave encouragement and other practical help as I put this book together, and I'm glad for the chance to thank them publicly. First, Rick Christian and all the other editors and staff at Focus on the Family have been a pleasure to work with. Their interest and diligence made this all happen.

Teresa Baier, my secretary, has been efficient and indispensable, as always.

And Ron DiCianni, a greatly talented illustrator, did a wonderful job with the front cover.

Thanks to each of you!

To Mom (Mrs. Dorothy Adkins),
who took all nine of us to church,
where we first heard the Bible stories;

Carmel,
whose prayer and walk encouraged
me to follow Jesus;

Walter Schewe,
whom God used to show me the power of love
and the ministry of the Holy Spirit;

and Norman,
who taught me much about myself
and will always be my friend

Contents

1. West Frankfort, Illinois 7
2. That's Weird Norman! 15
3. Food for Thought 27
4. My Beautiful Gold Chair 33
5. The Haunted House 41
6. Who's the Weird One? 47
7. Fixing Norman's Home 55
8. Searching for an Audience 61
9. Take Me Out to the Ball Game 71
10. The Eyes of a Child 79
11. Splish, Splash 85
12. An Unforgettable Vacation 93
13. Norman's New Birth 101
14. Learning to Love 109
15. Quiet Courage 127
16. Gangrene of the Soul 135
17. Anything but That! 143
18. God's Yes to Me 151
19. Discerning God's Will 157
20. On the Road of Faith 165
21. Evidence of Blessing 177
22. Dad's Homegoing 185
23. My Friend, the TV Star 191
24. Norman's Life Today 197
25. Thank You, Lord, for Norman 205

West Frankfort is a mining town in a part of southern Illinois known as "Little Egypt." Most people are surprised to learn there's coal in Illinois, but there is—a rich vein called Illinois Number Six that helps make our state a major coal producer. The land here opens out in expansive fields bordered by forested hills. The farmers grow corn, soybeans, and a little milo (a grain used for cattle feed).

The area got its name from the way the spring rains cause the Ohio and Mississippi rivers to flood the low-lying fields, much as the Nile floods the farmland of Egypt. The rising waters sink the land from view, leaving a chain of tree-studded islands. In the fall, our most pleasant season, the leaves turn russet, lemon, and gold. Once harvesting is out of the way, you can walk the fields with your shotgun and knock down a pheasant.

The first white people came here for the farming, back when Illinois was considered part of the western frontier. The towns mostly came later, with the mines. A good part of the population emigrated from different parts of Europe in the early 1900s.

Like most of the mining towns, West Frankfort has one main street, along which sit a handful of nineteenth-century brick buildings, bracketed now with gas stations and convenience stores. The Catholic church with its spire reminds many of the "old country." The marquee on the recently abandoned movie house bears a few letters from the title of the last show to play there. Like many downtown businesses, it lost its customers as shopping centers in outlying areas opened up.

The town is halved by the railroad tracks, which are still heavily trafficked in our community. Black cars with their black mounds of coal roll northeast toward Chicago or northwest toward St. Louis. When those trains rumble through, the whole town is reminded of the underground world in which so many of us spend our working lives.

Many of the towns in our area were built by one ethnic group or another, such as Slavs, Germans, or Italians. The people came here with the opening of the mines and prospered with them. But in the last forty years, many have moved away as technology has reduced the work force. I grew up with the feeling that life was getting steadily harder, more chancy.

As in all small towns, where everybody knows most everybody else, people in West Frankfort still care what others think of them. Your reputation in the community is an important issue.

In the neighborhoods, small, frame houses occupy lots that might accommodate houses twice or three times as large. Each house sits by itself, alone, withdrawn—as if protecting its secrets.

I've lived here all my life. My father worked as a manager in the mines. He believed in self-reliance and hard work. My mother's life was centered in the church— sometimes she even served as a guest preacher. She was gifted with spiritual insight and could convey clearly the forged-steel strength of her belief. She raised up her children, as the Bible says, "in the way they should go," and most of us haven't departed from it—though we've had to circle back around to it.

There were nine of us kids, six boys and

three girls. I came along right in the middle. I didn't think of our family as being poor, but I always knew my father's one great worry was keeping enough food on the table. Our large family and the closeness of the community made for a boyhood rich with playmates and high jinks. I loved playing baseball in the summer and sledding in the winter.

I had ambitions to be a singer, and I dropped out of college for good in my sophomore year to play in a rock 'n' roll band. My parents, not surprisingly, were against this. I went against them in many things in my life at that time, including my mother's Christianity.

Eventually I came home from touring with the band and resumed dating a girl I had gone out with in high school, Carmel Shelton. (She was named after an aunt, and since I was trying to win her over, I resisted the urge to make light of her unusual first name!) When I first met her, she wore white lipstick, which I wasn't sure my mother would like. But as I came to know Carmel, I discovered she was just the kind of girl my family wanted for me.

Several years after our first dates, when I returned from touring and looked for someone to marry, I thought of Carmel again. I knew I needed that kind of person. I courted her with everything I had, singing impromptu arias in "menu Italian" outside her window, sending flowers, and holding hands with her in the dark at the matinee. She fell for it and for me and became my wife on June 4, 1964.

Once Carmel and I married, I needed a well-paying job. Reluctant but determined to succeed, I went into the coal mines.

I remember my first ride down, descending that concrete shaft in the two-sided, metal elevator some seven hundred feet to the dark "streets" below. Breathing the air close to where the coal was actually being worked was overpowering. The dank smell filled my head and coated my throat. The blowers and other ventilation equipment didn't keep me from dreading black lung disease, from seeing in my mind's eye the men I knew who paused every few steps for breath, wheezing and coughing.

On the positive side, with the steady income I received from my job in the mines, Carmel and I began to build our life together. We had two children, Tracy and Tricia. We both started to mature. Even after I was married, I pursued my own ways for several years, but in 1968 I was born again. From that time on, I tried to live for the Lord. I worked at every task our church would give me, and I tried to be a good witness. Nothing I did really prepared me, however, for the way God wanted to teach me to love my neighbor as myself.

In 1973, Carmel and I bought our first home, moving in during the summer. We got a great deal on a two-story, white, frame house with a red brick and concrete porch. Built between 1910 and 1920, our new home needed a lot of work. That didn't bother me, though—I was young and dumb in those days. I couldn't wait to move in.

Over the next several months, I meant to restore both the house and its grounds. The house needed to be repainted and wallpapered throughout. It needed new carpeting. We also wanted to make the back porch, off the kitchen, into a breakfast nook with a bay window. The yard needed new plantings, and I was going to replace the old, over-grown shrubbery with trim plants in mulched beds. The brick porch needed to be tuck-pointed.

And then the patchy grass cried out for attention. I was going to take particular care with the lawn. My yard was going to look like a golf course when I finished!

When I surveyed what needed doing out in the yard, my first priority was to get rid of an old tree stump at the right-hand side in front, close to the street. I decided, not knowing any better, that I would take the one digging tool I owned—an oversized trowel—and dig around those roots until I could wrap a chain around the stump and pull it out with my car. When I filled in the hole, I would be well on my way to having my lawn looking like a fairway at the beautiful Augusta National Golf Club in Georgia, home of the Masters Tournament.

On the appointed day, I started digging. I had my coveralls on and was barefooted. At noon, the temperature had already risen into the eighties. My wife and girls had gone uptown, so I was left to myself with plenty of time, I thought, to complete the job. I dug for a while and started to discover how deep the roots went. This was going to take much longer than I had figured!

My mind started to wander. While I was digging, I had a chance to look around the neighborhood and consider my new neighbors. I was very gung ho about telling people about my faith. (I still am, but in a different way.) I wanted everyone to know that Billy Graham had moved in! To tell the truth, I wasn't sure any of my new neighbors needed evangelizing. Still, I wanted them to be aware of my commitment.

On my right was a Catholic family. I had never known a Catholic family really well, so I thought I'd watch them to see what they were like. On my left was a retired Methodist preacher. I was eager to discuss my views on the faith with him—I wanted to impress him particularly. (As it turned out, he was a man of great wisdom and became one of my dearest friends.) And straight across the street from me, directly in front of our door, was a widow lady named Marie.

That was about the neighborhood, except that next door to Marie's house—to my left as I looked across the street—was an old house that seemed abandoned. Large bushes had grown up around it. The front porch sagged. The windows were filthy. Chocolate-colored paint was falling off everywhere. I had never seen anyone use the front door. The grass looked as if someone still cut it occasionally, but no lawnmower had touched it recently. It was the kind of place we used to think of as haunted when we were children. It seemed to be hiding behind the limbs of a tall oak tree—like a person who's afraid covering himself with his arms.

You could see how dark it must be in there. You could imagine, even standing in the sunshine, ghostly drafts of cold air chasing each other. Just looking at it reminded me of the kind of dream in which you feel suffocated, you hear heavy footsteps, and you wait for the end. I was hoping someone would come along, tear the old place down, and put a nice, new home in there. That house gave me the creeps.

As I continued digging, the sweat now running down the sides of my face, mixing with the grime on my forearms, I saw someone come out of the haunted house. I couldn't believe my eyes. He had come out the back door—I was at enough of an angle to see him, the haunted house being separated from Marie's by a side lawn.

Then I recognized who it was. It was Norman! I thought, "Oh, no! God, that's weird Norman over there! How could You have me buy a house across the street from Norman?"

Norman Corbin was the odd, creepy guy every town seems to have. You're never quite sure whether he's dangerous or not, but you don't want to find out the hard way. I had known of Norman since grade school. He spent his days walking up and down Main Street twice as fast—or slow—as most folks, rubber galoshes, instead of shoes, flopping on his feet.

He was about six feet, two inches tall and sturdily built. He wore dirty overalls and a hat that was so grease- and oil-stained that you could hardly tell it had once been a fedora. Often on his rambles through town, Norman would stop, take off his hat, run his hand through his bushy, gray hair, look up at the sky, and shout, "Hey! Who-a? What'uv that bestin franguss? Dreet-mack cripno!" or some such nonsense. You wondered where the men in white coats were. I assumed he was crazy.

My wife and I had prayed about which house to buy, and I couldn't understand why the Lord would have led us to a house across the street from Norman. Tracy was eight and Tricia was five, and I couldn't always be there protecting them. I wanted them to be able to play in their own front yard without fear. So my immediate response to seeing Norman come around that corner was to feel betrayed by God.

I watched Norman and thought, "He really is strange!" He didn't notice me for a while because he was tinkering with a gas-powered lawn mower, trying to start it. He pulled the cord several times without success, and then he started marching around it as if the lawn mower were his prisoner and he was threatening it with torture.

Suddenly he saw me, and next he did something I *really* couldn't believe. He raised his arms like the Incredible Hulk and screamed at me, "Yeeaaoow!"

Then he charged down the side of his house with his hands and arms raised up as if he were about to cross the street and strangle me. He was screaming all the time, "Yeeaaoow! Aarggh!"

My lower jaw dropped in amazement, and I felt a surge of adrenaline that had nothing to do with working hard. My heart was beating as if I'd just run a hundred-yard dash. Fortunately, Norman stopped just short of the street. He glowered at me, keeping his arms raised. I froze, not knowing whether to run or prepare to defend myself. Actually, I was so paralyzed by fear that I doubt I could've run.

Unsure what to expect next, I watched Norman do what I least expected. He simply turned and went back to his lawn mower.

Well, needless to say, by this time he had my attention! I remember thinking, "God, I know we're supposed to love everybody, but if he comes over here, I'm going to defend myself!" I gripped the tool in my hand more tightly.

I looked again, and here came Norman rushing at me once more! "Aarggh! Aarggh!" he yelled.

He did that three times in all, each time

stopping on his side of the street, staring at me, and going back to his lawn mower.

Then something happened to me that I expected about as much as I had expected Norman's behavior. A feeling seemed to settle down on me that lifted me up as it fell. It was like a misty rain, fresh like that, and at the same time peaceful and quiet like fog. I don't mean something I could see. I'm trying to find a way to describe the presence of God.

And with that presence, a boldness came to me that I don't normally have. Suddenly I knew I was going to go talk to Norman. I would still be wary, but I had the assurance that if I stayed on my toes, I would be OK. I almost wanted to pause and relish the feeling, the *lift* of operating out of a confidence beyond my own. Faith prompted me that now was the time, and I stood up from where I was digging around the tree stump and walked across the street and into Norman's yard.

I walked right up to him; I had never been that close to him before. His eyes looked huge behind the thick lenses of his glasses. He needed a shave, and he needed to look in the mirror when he *did* shave, because the stubble of his white beard, present everywhere, was almost shaggy in patches.

His downcast eyes searched the grass as if a missing lawn mower part might be lying around somewhere. He switched his weight from one foot to the other like a nervous animal that wants to break out of its confinement. His hands clenched on the lawn mower's handle, and I had the feeling he would have swung it over his head and smashed it on the ground if he had had the strength. Actually, since he was so big, I wasn't sure he couldn't have done it.

I said, "Are you having trouble with your lawn mower, Norman?"

He looked at me with those huge eyes and said, "Are you having trouble with your lawn mower, Norman?"

I thought, "Didn't I just say that?" Why was he repeating me? His voice was gruff and low, with a reedy rumble in it, like the sound you produce by blowing on a thick blade of grass between your thumbs.

"Well, Norman," I continued, "I'm not much of a lawn mower mechanic, but let me see what I can do here."

I bent down to tighten the screws of the housing and clean the spark plug. As I did so, I heard him say, "I'm not much of a lawn mower mechanic, Norman, but let me see what I can do here."

I *didn't* know much about lawn mowers. What would this man think of me if I failed to help him? How would he react? I prayed as I worked, wiping the spark plug clean and putting it back in. When I pulled the cord once more, the mower started as if it had just come back from the repair shop. It sat there and purred.

Norman looked at the lawn mower, at me, at my house, back at me, and at the mower once more. I didn't know what he was going to do. His eyes stopped switching from one thing to another. He stepped back, looked off in an embarrassed way, and got this great big grin on his face. I saw a green-and-yellow tooth here, a green-and-yellow tooth there, and two more down below.

As I went back across the street, I thought, "Maybe that grin is the start of a friendship." I had the feeling that something significant might have happened in my life—quiet but important. Our encounter didn't square with my previous notions of Norman. He was someone other than the person I had taken him to be, although who he really was remained a mystery.

The next few times I saw Norman on our street, I called out, "Hi," and he waved back and said hello before flapping off down the street in his galoshes.

Chapter 3

FOOD FOR THOUGHT

"With all the church people in town, surely someone had witnessed to Norman, but then most of those same church people were seated in that little restaurant with him, pretending they didn't see him."

In our town, a lot of folks used to go to the Dairy Queen after church on Sunday nights. It was tradition. The members of the churches that had forty-five-minute services got there first, bought their ice cream, and sat down. Then came folks from the churches that had the fifty-minute services. The Baptists, Presbyterians, Methodists, and everybody else went there.

The members of the different churches always waved and greeted one another the same way:

"Hi, Bill."

"Hi, John."

"Hi, Betty."

"How's your family?"

"Fine."

"How was your church?"

"Oh, wonderful."

No one in our town, it seemed, ever had a bad church service. And guess who always walked into the middle of all that? Norman. How he got the money to pay for his ice cream, I wasn't sure. I had seen him mowing another person's lawn since our encounter; maybe he made money that way.

How did we treat him? We acted as if we didn't see him. And Mike Adkins avoided him as much as anyone else. I've often wondered why we acted like that. I suppose none of us wanted to be thought strange, to be excluded, and talking to Norman posed the risk of being grouped with someone who was so clearly an outcast.

One Sunday night during the early fall after the tree stump episode, however, I was seated with Carmel at the Dairy Queen when Norman came in. Seeing him, I thought about the seed of friendship that had been planted between us. I felt the Lord was telling me to go over and talk to him. I had also been wondering if anyone had ever told Norman about Jesus—witnessed to him. With all the church people in town, surely someone had, but then most of those same church people were seated in that little restaurant with him, pretending they didn't see him.

I remember watching how the girls behind the counter treated Norman that night. They didn't mistreat him, but they acted as if they were frightened of him. Norman clearly needed a friend. Still, I didn't want to go over and greet him, because I was afraid of what my neighbors might think. But finally, after asking Carmel to pray for me, I went anyway.

Norman was seated at a booth close to the counter. Trying to hide what I was doing, I walked up and bought another ice cream cone, then quickly slipped into the booth opposite him.

I looked at him and was shocked once more at how dirty he was. He kept his oil-soaked hat on, and his eyes struck me again as looking huge through the thick glasses. His left ear, squashed by the hat, had a big splotch of dirt on it. His ice cream had smeared into his whiskers near his mouth.

I kept my voice low and spoke quickly. "Do you remember who I am, Norman?" I said.

"Do you remember who I am?" he repeated.

"I'm your neighbor."

"I'm your neighbor."

If he was going to repeat everything I said, this was going to take all night! I cut to the point. "Norman, do you know who Jesus is?"

"Do you know who Jesus is?"

"Did you ever think about asking Jesus to come into your heart and be your Savior and your Lord?"

I was expecting him to repeat that, too, or part of it, but he was silent now. He studied me for a long moment, his eyes intent. Finally he lowered his ice cream and said, "I've given it serious consideration."

I was stunned—surprised, to be honest, that he had the mental ability to comprehend what I was asking. Maybe I expected to discover he couldn't grasp spiritual issues and my responsibility would be at an end. Maybe I was looking for an out.

I didn't know what to say, so I didn't say anything. I was so surprised that I simply went back to my wife. I had to think now about who Norman really was and what friendship with him might mean.

Chapter 4

MY BEAUTIFUL
GOLD CHAIR

*"Although Norman had
dressed for the occasion, he
hadn't bathed for it."*

One day a few weeks later, I saw Norman out in his yard again. It seemed to me that we should take the next step as friends, that I should invite him over to my house. I resisted the idea, though. Carmel had been fixing up our place so that the interior now looked like something out of a magazine. We had painted the living room white. Most of the furniture had the graceful lines of light, early American cabinetry. It was hard for me to see Norman in the picture. Also, I didn't know what I would say to him. And then I remembered that there was going to be a Christian special on TV, a concert of gospel songs.

So I called out, "Norman!"

He looked up from the grass bag he was trying to attach to his lawn mower and smiled at me. After I'd talked with him in the Dairy Queen, he had begun reacting to me in a much more normal way.

"We want to invite you to come over to our house to watch television tonight," I shouted. "Six-thirty."

I didn't know if he would come or not. He looked at me and went, "Uh-huh."

Then I told Carmel what I had done. Many wives would have been nervous about hosting such an event, if not outright angry with their husbands for having invited such a guest. But Carmel was just as intent on being a good witness as I was. And she is, by nature, more generous. From the beginning, really, she was more than supportive of my efforts with Norman. Her only criticism came through her silences when she thought I wasn't doing enough.

As it began to get dark around 6:30, I started looking out the window to see if Norman was coming. Before long, I spotted him walking along the side of his house where he had performed his Incredible Hulk act. As he came closer, I could see he had gotten all dressed up for us. He had put on a tie that hung at an angle across his chest and stomach, off to one side.

When I opened our door, I said, "Well,

Norman, come on in. We're glad to see you!" That was, in part, a lie. Although he had dressed for the occasion, he hadn't *bathed* for it. And with his poor eyes, there was going to be only one good place for him to sit in front of my color TV—*in my chair*.

I love my chair! It's a light gold, covered with a velvety fabric—a gorgeous recliner. I love to crank it out and drift off to sleep in front of the TV in the evenings. I was sure Norman was going to soil it.

Nevertheless, I sat him down in it and gave it a little crank to elevate his feet. This startled him, but then he liked the feeling.

Carmel and I sat farther back from the TV, to one side, on the couch. We watched the musical special, and we watched Norman watching it. He sat so still, hardly breathing, that we could see how involved he had become in the program.

While I watched the musical groups with their spangled costumes and fussed-over hairstyles, I thought of my own ambitions to be an entertainer, first as a rock 'n' roll star, and right then as a Christian singer, just like the people we were watching.

About the last thing I had done as an entertainer was to sing at Ridgecrest, a national Baptist campground. I had gone there as a counselor with our youth group. One night there was a talent show that was really for the kids, but I was pressed into service, too.

I performed the act I used to do in nightclubs, giving impersonations of different singers such as Louis Armstrong, Elvis, Johnny Ray, and the Platters. I could really get up on the high notes of the Platters' big hit "Only You." I told them that when I performed this same act in nightclubs, it almost ruined my life, but then I had found Jesus and a whole new way of life. At the end, they gave Jesus a standing ovation. The way people responded that night made me feel that maybe God would have me use my talents full-time in the ministry. But episodes like this came and went, and I was still laboring in the coal mines.

At the end of the television program, Norman got up and said, "Thank you very much." That was all. I walked him over to the door, saw him down the steps (they've always been tricky—they're too narrow), and watched him cross my yard. "Good night, Norman," I said. "Come back again." He was headed for that dark, forbidding house, and I thought again of how nice Carmel had made our home. This time, instead of not being able to see him in the picture, I found it difficult to let him go back to his own world.

I will admit, though, that when I came back into the living room, I examined my chair for damage. It was a miracle. There wasn't a single mark on it! Carmel sprayed with an air freshener, and we could hardly tell Norman had been there. In the important ways, though, we knew he had.

Chapter 5

THE HAUNTED HOUSE

"I wondered apprehensively whether Norman would want how he lived to be exposed to another person."

In those days, Carmel and I visited people in their homes to tell them about a new Sunday school class at the church. We followed up leads given to us by the head of the church's education department, asking young married couples whether they would like to join us on Sunday mornings. During these visits, we spoke about our faith, witnessing to the non-Christians we met.

A short while after we had invited Norman over to watch the TV special, I decided that since I was talking with people in their homes about the Lord, maybe I ought to visit Norman the same way. In his own words, he had given becoming a

Christian "serious consideration," and I thought I might be used of the Lord to help him finally decide to do so.

The whole house had a dark feel to it. And as I approached Norman's door for the first time one spring evening, in the failing light, I wondered apprehensively whether he would want how he lived to be exposed to another person.

After I knocked, Norman showed me in. I thought I had prepared myself for the worst, but I still could hardly believe how filthy his living quarters were. There was dirt everywhere, on every surface—every table, bookshelf, and chair. I brushed against the curtain by the door in the living room, and dust rained down. I noticed the windows especially. As far as you could tell looking through them, it was pitch dark outside, for the windows were so dirty—on the inside as well as the outside—that they let in very little light.

Norman invited me into his kitchen, where, without offering me anything, he took a moldy carton out of the refrigerator and drank down a gulp of what must have been horribly curdled milk.

The floor was so dirty that you couldn't tell how the linoleum was patterned. The light fixture had been converted into an out-let, and an extension cord snaked out of it. This extension cord ran into a multiple-plug adapter that had a swarm of other cords running out of it and into various appliances and fixtures in the kitchen and the whole back section of the house. What a fire trap that place was!

Open cans of spaghetti, ravioli, and tuna fish covered the aluminum table and the counter space next to the sink. Forks and spoons sprouted out of their tops, and I realized Norman must have eaten all his meals out of those cans, cold.

Besides these impressions of neglect, I had a strong sense that I had stepped back in time. The furnishings of the house came from the 1920s. The kitchen cupboard had a flour bin in it with a sifter. There was an old Victrola in the living room that you had to hand wind. It was as if Norman lived in a forgotten world.

I remember especially his lumpy, unmade bed, the cold and mildewing covers he threw over himself each night. The weather was starting to warm up that spring (we had passed the winter since the Dairy Queen episode), but the house must have been terribly cold for him those last few months. (Just how cold I wouldn't find out until later, when I experienced firsthand how poorly his coal-burning furnace worked.)

We went back into the living room, and I told him I didn't mean to intrude upon him, but I thought that every once in a while, if he didn't mind, I would come and talk to him.

And that's what I did. He became less nervous and shy as he grew accustomed to seeing me, although he still kept his eyes downcast when he muttered replies to my questions. We talked about his background. He told me he had lived with his mother until her death some ten years before. Besides cutting lawns in the summer, he made his money from cleaning furnaces in the winter.

I learned I wasn't the only neighbor interested in Norman, either. Marie, the woman next door, handled his finances. She also owned his house and let him live in it without charge (a condition of the transfer of ownership from Norman's mother to her, but an act of love, too).

Norman never repeated what I said anymore, and I could tell he liked the visits. At least once during each of our times together, he would throw back his great head with its tousled, dirty, gray hair and let me see that four-tooth, jack-o'-lantern grin.

My relationship with Norman progressed slowly. I didn't understand much of his behavior, and it took me a couple of months before I stopped being a little afraid of him. A butcher knife, its blade bigger than your wrist, lay on his kitchen table, and I kept wondering in my early visits whether he might still do something crazy. At times, when Norman acted skittish, his moods changing abruptly, I could almost hear the "thunk" of that knife being plunged into my back.

These fears persisted partly because of a confrontation I had on the street with a confused man who thought of himself as a prophet. The week after I spoke with Norman

at the Dairy Queen, this man walked up to
me on the sidewalk in front of the local grocery store, Sawicki's. He glared at me and
warned me not to have anything to do with
Norman. He said that Norman was demon-
possessed, that he might harm me, and that
the Lord had reached out to Norman time
and again and had finally abandoned him to
the devil.

I knew this man casually. And he
seemed so confident of what he was saying
that he shook me. (This was the era of the
movie *The Exorcist,* too, and many people,
in the church and out, were talking about
demons.)

No one in town knew what was wrong
with Norman, not really. But you hear the
rumors about such things down at the bar-
bershop, especially in a small town like
ours. Men there occasionally speculated
about what Norman's problem might be. I
heard a guy say one time, "I know what it is.
He was hit by a Greyhound bus."

Another fellow said, "No, that's not it at
all. He was really a genius, but then he got
so much knowledge stuffed into his head
that his mind just exploded one day."

That sounded silly, but it reminded me of
a teacher I had in junior high. He really
knew his subject, but every day he came to
school with his tie on inside out. At the time,
I had figured that maybe he knew so much

about what he taught that it crowded everything else out of his brain.

Yet another theory was that Norman was
an *idiot savant*, a person who's mentally
defective generally but has a special genius
in a particular field. I remember children
used to poke Norman and scream out a
series of numbers, and he would yell out a
great-big number as if he had added their
numbers together.

Mockery like this, once I thought about
it, told me that other people were afraid of
Norman as well. You don't pester a person
who doesn't disturb you.

I felt, though, that the Lord had called
me to minister to Norman, and I was determined to carry through. I kept going over
to see him in the early evenings. But I did
watch him carefully. Sometimes I would be
standing off to one side while Norman
shuffled around in the kitchen. He would
glance over at me and catch me looking at
him suspiciously. I know this frightened
him, but I couldn't always disguise my
own fears.

Late in the fall, I decided I would perform
a kind of exorcism on Norman—just in case.
I remember it was one of those gray, wet days
in November, and as I walked across the
street to his house, I had a powerful impression once again of icy drafts chasing each
other through his halls. It made me wonder

what evil I might stir up in Norman's soul that day.

After asking me in, Norman followed me into the living room to watch TV. We often carried on our conversations with one program or another going in the background. A few minutes into my visit, when I had screwed up my courage and the program had Norman's attention, I circled behind him. He was seated in a rocking chair, and I moved toward him to put my hands around the back of his head.

Don't ask me where I got my ideas about how to do an exorcism. I wasn't about to do anything as fancy as I had seen in the movies. But I thought that if my heart were in the right place, God would honor whatever gestures I made.

I was still a few feet from Norman when my tiptoe steps started to make the floorboards creak. He shuffled in his chair as if he might turn around, so I backed off.

About a half hour later, in the middle of the next show, I snuck up on him again, slowly, testing the floorboards with each step before completely transferring my weight. I remember how dark the house was because of the gray sky and the filthy windows, and I felt again the presence of a sort of spiritual darkness.

My palms were sweating, and I didn't know what to expect when at last I stood

Chapter
7

FIXING
NORMAN'S HOME

*"When I had finished
painting, cleaning, and
wiring, I felt I still hadn't
improved the place all that
much. It didn't strike me
as even livable."*

directly behind him. I waited till the volume of the TV program rose, the music of a chase scene building. Then I quickly put my hands around the back of his head, inches from his scalp, and prayed, whispering, "You come out! You come out!"

Norman turned toward me, and I thought I might see a face distorted by evil. I jerked my hands back as if he were a hot stove. But instead he gave me an open, questioning look that seemed to say, "What in the *world* are you doing?"

The blood seemed to drain out of my head, and the tension went from my muscles. Immediately I felt silly. His sincere look made me realize I was the one acting strangely.

Pretending I hadn't said or done anything unusual, I looked away, stepped to the side, and tried to appear deep in thought. Norman was so trusting, I realized then. He was the one taking the risk, letting me come into his home when so many people in his life had abused him. From that day on my fears abated, and I came to admire Norman more and more.

There was spiritual darkness in that house, though. Partly it was in Norman, but a lot of it was in me, too.

At the beginning, the way things went with Norman, I would get really pleased with what I had done, and then the Lord would ask me to do something else—put a challenge in front of me that seemed the thing to do. I got to looking at Norman's house and comparing it to how nice Carmel had made our place, and I realized no one was there to make things nice for Norman.

The walls in his house were tea colored from water stains, and much of the wallpaper was peeling off. Long strips hung down from the ceiling in several places. So I bought gallons of white and blue paint and set to work painting the interior. After that, I painted the outside of the house.

When I finished these jobs, Norman's house still seemed dark somehow, and while painting the place, I had a chance to think about other projects that needed doing. I started in on some of these, cleaning the kitchen floor so that the brick design of the linoleum appeared again, redoing some wiring to eliminate the fire hazard in the kitchen and elsewhere. Carmel helped me as much as she could, which was a lot. In the course of my friendship with Norman, she assisted me at every turn.

Enough time elapsed between the jobs I did for Norman that I really didn't have to neglect my family to help him. In fact, my girls were beginning to think of Norman as a family favorite. They had come to know him, after all, as a neighbor, not a freak.

When I had finished painting, cleaning, and wiring, I felt I still hadn't improved the place all that much. It didn't strike me as even livable. At that point I almost lost heart. The job seemed too big for me. I told God, "This is too big! I can't do this! It's too big, God!"

We were into the winter then, and one day a blizzard hit our town. The state police directed people off the nearby interstate, which had become impassable, and housed them temporarily in school gymnasiums and church basements.

Chapter 8

SEARCHING FOR AN AUDIENCE

"Norman couldn't express his gratitude very well. So I felt other people should know what I was doing and appreciate my good deeds."

The help of those people from the Methodist church was great, but working with Norman got to be a thankless job. Norman couldn't express his gratitude very well. He seemed to feel that someone named Mike had bumbled into his life and decided to help out, and that was fine. If I had bumbled out of his life, though, I wasn't sure he would have missed me much. So I felt other people should know what I was doing and appreciate my good deeds.

One night at a high-school basketball game, during halftime, I was standing on the wood floor beside the bleachers, drinking a Coke with my brother and several mutual friends. They were talking about playing more man-to-man defense and doubling down on our opponent's big man.

Right in the middle of the discussion, I said, "Hey, you know what? I'm helping Norman."

They all looked at me for a moment. Then my brother said rather nonchalantly, "That's nice, Mike." Turning slowly and purposefully, he said to one of the men standing with us, "Usually you want to smother their big guy with a zone, but they shoot too well from the outside. They can really put it up."

I knew then that I had better put it up, too. When was I going to learn? In fact, I may have started to learn from the experience, really learn from it, right then. I saw that I was hardly loving my neighbor as myself. And I started to question why I had ever befriended Norman in the first place.

I was sure I had felt a prompting from the Lord to cross the street and talk to Norman. God had given me the courage to walk into the arms of that bearlike man. I came to see, though, once I thought about it, that I was inclined that way for reasons that had as much to do with me as with Norman. (As I've often said since then, I went across the street to clean up an old hermit, and God used him to clean *me* up.)

When I moved into the neighborhood, I

The people who helped with the relief effort at the Methodist church underwent a kind of revival at that time. One of the results was that they got more excited than ever about reaching out to others. And to this day I don't know who, but someone told these Methodists about my efforts with Norman.

That weekend, about twenty people from the Methodist church showed up at our door with mops, brooms, and vacuum cleaners. Thank God for the Methodists! "We've come to help you clean and fix up Norman's house," they said, and so they did.

Over the next two weekends, the men and women of that group worked like all get-out. The women did a thorough job of cleaning the house. Norman was something of a pack rat, collecting anything and everything. The first time I saw his bathtub, it was filled to the brim with paper bags. Those women helped me clear out a lot of stuff and organize what Norman insisted on keeping. They also took the venetian blinds to the car wash and helped me wash the windows, inside and out. (Yes, we washed the windows in the dead of winter. The weather after the storm, as sometimes happens, was exceptionally fine.)

Norman was delighted with the changes, although he never did much to help. He stood around and watched. I remember his watching me cleaning the windows in particular. He must have thought before that he lived in a house with permanently stained glass, because he looked shocked to see the light pour through when the windows were cleaned.

The men helped me continue my wiring projects and put in a new floor in the bathroom. They also worked on the plumbing in the attic, where, through the process of putting in a new floor, we traced a problem with the water heater. They repaired chairs and tables that were on their last legs, and they replaced rotting boards out on the back porch.

Those folks did an amazing amount of work in two days. They seemed to enjoy it. When they left, I sat back and thought how much Christians can accomplish when they work together.

was intent on living for the Lord, and that included witnessing to those I met. I wanted people to see how dedicated I was, thinking that if people saw what I was doing, they would have a good example for going on with God as Carmel and I were doing. So I wanted what I did to be noticed for what I thought of as good reasons. Looking back on it now, I can see that I was actually trying to win God's approval— playing to an audience.

My dad gave the most apt description of me. Once he was trying to describe me to another man, and he said, "This boy, it's like he's been chasing something all his life, and whatever it is, he hasn't caught it yet." Even after becoming a Christian, I still hadn't.

What was I chasing? That's hard to say, but strange as it may sound, maybe a way of saying it is that I dreamed of playing baseball. I loved baseball first and last, and I would have played professionally if I hadn't been running in quicksand around the bases—I just had no speed. I rarely solved the mysteries of the curveball, either. I loved the game, though; I loved expressing myself that way.

Once I figured out I would never play professional baseball, I found a substitute in music. As I mentioned earlier, I dropped out of college in the middle of my sophomore year and started touring with a rock 'n' roll band, The Percussions. We played a slew of honky-tonks throughout the South, including Porky's nightclub in Fort Lauderdale, Florida, the place they made the movies about.

One week we would eat peanut butter, and the next we would eat steak. We played for one owner who wouldn't pay us, and when we pulled out on him, he threatened to have us killed—he called us at our next stop and told us he was sending his boys over. We went through a lot of fun and excitement in those days.

I was more ambitious than the others, and when I tired of traveling, I thought of other ways to promote my career. I've always believed in the direct approach, so one day I walked into the RCA studios in Nashville, introduced myself, and said I had a tape I'd like to play for them. I had written and recorded a song on home equipment that I thought a new TV series about space invaders might be interested in using.

The secretary seemed to think I was a relative of Chet Atkins, and since he was the head of RCA in Nashville, she sent me right on back. I met Chet's assistant, Bob Ferguson, and he listened to my tape. He liked it and thought we might have something with the TV show tie-in. And just like that, I had a recording contract with RCA!

I remember thinking how I was going to

be on the same record label as Elvis Presley. The studio in which he recorded his early hits was right next to where I met with Bob Ferguson. For a little while, the world seemed bright, the streets paved with gold.

We did four recording sessions, and RCA backed me with everything it had, including a twenty-six-piece orchestra. I recorded Glen Campbell- and Bobby Goldsboro-type songs: upbeat ballads.

Nothing came of it. They couldn't give a record to anyone, let alone sell any of them. Naturally, I grew very discouraged.

Then I had an opportunity to audition for "The Joey Bishop Show" at the Du Quoin State Fair near where we live. At least I *thought* I did. Louis Armstrong was to play there, and the fair people arranged it so that Armstrong would bring me up on stage as if I were just someone out of the audience, and then I would sing with his band. A guy from the ABC Booking Corporation in Chicago would listen and decide whether he wanted me for Joey Bishop.

I was all dressed up in my suit, ready to go on, when Armstrong's personal manager put a stop to it. He had never heard me sing, and he wouldn't allow the possibility that Louis Armstrong might be embarrassed. I couldn't blame him, although I was extremely disappointed once again.

Only two days after that, I did sing at a

private party given for the stars who played the fair. Waylon Jennings and Jessie Colter were there. The head of the organizing committee gave the party at his mansion.

I sang well that night. Everyone seemed to enjoy it. And then I stayed for a while, long enough to see the drunken goings-on. I remember a beautiful girl sitting at the piano in a bikini, weaving and bobbing with a sea of alcohol in her system, slurring out, "Just a Closer Walk with Thee."

As I drove home that night, I was in despair. The stars loved my singing, but I couldn't get anybody else to listen. I had the terrible feeling that something supernatural was preventing my success. At that point I cried out to God, "If it's just a matter of being stubborn, God, I can do that. But if You're the one stopping this, I know I can't defeat You. That's an impossibility. A man must yield to You, and if You're preventing my success, show me."

I knew He was alive. I had no doubt about that, but I hadn't been serving Him. The truth was, I preferred not having anything much to do with Him. I had vowed to my mother, in the midst of my adolescent rebellion, that once I was out of her control I would never go to church again.

Within the next twenty-four hours, RCA canceled my recording contract. I knew God had answered my prayer. Before this, it was as if I had known only rumors of God's existence, but then I saw Him in action, and I knew He wanted me on another path.

Yet I didn't know what that could be. I was twenty-seven years old. My hopes seemed at an end. I was working in the coal mines of my hometown, and it didn't look as though I'd ever get out. I was at the lowest point of my life. I wasn't suicidal, but I understood how others became that way.

God then moved in a positive way. People, especially Southern Baptists, started witnessing to me everywhere I would go— in the grocery store, at the softball field. I honestly think the Southern Baptists in town got together and decided to take out after me!

A successful doctor who went to the Southern Baptist church asked me to his house one Saturday. He knew I loved sports, and he saw the condition of my life clearly, so he said exactly the right words: "Mike, I think you're very unhappy, and God wants to quarterback your life." I was surprised at how those two short thoughts addressed my situation so fully. He went on, "I'm not a theologian, but I think if we look at the Bible together and you're willing to accept Christ, not only as Savior, but also as the Lord of your life—the leader, the quarterback— great things are possible."

And so, seven years before I met Norman,

I accepted the Lord. I had been trying to live for Him ever since. When I realized, though, how much I wanted to be applauded for helping Norman, I understood how persistent old habits can be and how they can disguise themselves and reappear in unexpected ways. For I was still trying to be a performer, still trying to win the applause of the audience. I hadn't learned to accept God's love as grace—something I didn't win by virtue of my actions, but a love I received by virtue of who God is.

After bragging at the basketball game, I thought of the first time I met Norman. I guess I had expected helping him to be easy, painless. But that was about as realistic as expecting to dig out that tree stump with a trowel.

I saw Norman out in his yard one day that next summer, and it suddenly occurred to me that I had never done anything with him just for fun. The idea that he might be a baseball fan intrigued me, so I went over to talk with him. "Hey, Norman," I said, "are you a baseball fan? Do you root for the Redbirds?"

Norman just sort of grinned to himself.

"No, I mean it, Norman," I said. "Have you ever been to see the St. Louis Cardinals play?"

"No. Like to. I see 'em on television," he said.

"Why don't we go to a game, then?" I said. "I'll get tickets. You wait and see if I don't."

I bought tickets and arranged to meet Norman the morning of the game. We would have about a ninety-mile drive northwest to St. Louis.

Norman came out to the car the day of the game wearing a heavy, tweed overcoat. I told him to go back in the house and put it away. It was mid-July, and the temperature at midmorning promised that the day would be a scorcher. Norman loped back to his house saying he had to check the lock anyway, but he returned still wearing the coat. I sent him back again, and he remembered some equipment he needed to put away in the back. When he returned, he was *still* in the coat. This happened several times, with Norman thinking of something else to do each time he went to the house, and he never did get rid of the tweed overcoat. I was afraid we wouldn't get out of his driveway, so instead of insisting that he put away the coat, I finally got out and held the door for him the next time he approached the car.

We had no more than left the city limits when I noticed that Norman's eyes were glued to the CB radio on the dashboard. "Norman, have you ever talked on a CB?" I asked.

Norman shook his head, so I flipped the switch to channel 19 and enjoyed watching his interest and amusement at the truckers' lively chatter. I finally asked Norman if he would like to talk on the radio and added for encouragement, "You just push that button and talk, Norman!"

I took the mike and said, "Hey, breaker, we've got a fellow here who's never had a CB, never been around one before. He mows lawns around our town for a living, and he cleans ashes out of the furnaces in the wintertime. Let's give him a handle."

Somebody said, "Well, he'd be the Old Grasscutter."

I handed the microphone back to Norman. He took it and said, "Hello? This is Old Grasscutter."

Several people responded, and Norman was clearly fascinated. He remained absorbed with the CB for the entire trip to St. Louis, which gave me time to reflect. It was as if the CB had given him a connection somehow, a way to relate to and enjoy other people. It was difficult for me to try to put myself in Norman's galoshes and understand how lonely and frustrating his life must be at times. I wondered what it would be like to have everyone think you weren't normal.

I recalled once more how the little kids would come up to him, poke him in the ribs, and shout out numbers. I thought I knew Norman well enough now to ask him what he thought of the children's doing that.

Norman said something I'll always remember: "Oh, I don't know, Mike. I guess

I always thought they were kind of crazy."

That just about summed up Norman's relationships and made me all the more happy that we were on our way to the ball park.

When we arrived at the Busch Stadium parking lot, I angled the car into the space, opened the door, and was hit with a blast of ovenlike heat. Right then I decided that while I hadn't been able to talk Norman out of his itchy, tweed overcoat when we left his house, I would just have to be firm now. It was ridiculous for him to go into the stadium with that thing on. "Norman," I said, "if you don't leave the coat in the car, we're going home right now."

He looked at me and could tell I meant business, so he reluctantly took off the coat and handed it to me. I threw it in the back seat, locked the door, and turned around to see him walking toward the stadium.

Then I saw why he had been wearing that long coat. Oh, my goodness! He had on two pairs of dress pants, one on top of the other, and both were ripped all the way up the back! "Norman," I called, "come over here for a minute." He walked back. "Let's put your coat on you," I said.

We put his coat on him and headed in to the ball game. When we went through the turnstile, the first guy who passed us was bebopping along with a big transistor radio in one hand—a boom box—and a drink in the other. He had Brillo pad hair and wore cutoffs and a T-shirt—one of those guys who doesn't have a muscle on his body but thinks he does and wants to show off. He didn't give Norman, in his long, hot overcoat, a second look. But as he walked by me, his bebopping slowed, and he gave *me* the once-over!

Norman and I went inside, found our seats, and sat down. As the game started, I asked Norman if he liked baseball. But Norman wasn't watching the game at all. He was looking at the people.

"I've never seen this many people in one place before," he said. There were almost thirty thousand in the stands that day. "I was only out of town once in my whole life before this. Went thirty miles one time."

"Well, yeah, there's a lot of people, Norman, but watch the game," I said. I pointed toward the diamond. "Look, the Cardinals have a guy on first. He might steal!"

But Norman wasn't going to watch. The crowd distracted him too much.

I focused my attention on the game for a moment, but I soon noticed that Norman was watching the concession man weave his way up and down the stands, selling hot dogs. "Oh, Norman, do you want a hot dog?" I asked. "For some reason, hot dogs are better at the ball game than anywhere else."

He wanted one, with a little mustard.

Then he wanted another. A few minutes later, he decided to try two more. Before the end of the third inning, I had bought him soft drinks, peanuts, popcorn, nacho cheese chips, and ice cream—practically everything they sold at the ball park except beer. The trash around our feet looked as if we had fed all the animals at the zoo!

Norman's appetite at last appeased, I noticed he was beginning to perspire heavily and told him to slip out of his coat while we were sitting down. He did and immediately looked more comfortable. I went back to watching the game, a good, close contest. Norman went back to watching the people and looking out for the hot dog man.

Before we knew it, it was time for the seventh-inning stretch. Completely forgetting about his pants, I said, "Norman, let's stand up and stretch. See, everyone is doing it. Let's stretch. It feels good!"

As we stretched, I happened to glance behind me, and I saw that the eyes of the guys right in back of us were growing bigger by the second. They stared at Norman, astonished. "OK, Norman," I said hurriedly, "time to sit down now."

That evening, reflecting on the day, I told my wife, "I had a lot of fun with Norman today. I really did!" It occurred to me that a day like that was what Christians really ought to do—just reach out to somebody.

Chapter
10

THE EYES OF
A CHILD

*"Norman had an unusual
capacity to be absorbed in
the scene before him — to
really see everything."*

Then came a period through the next year when I became even more personally involved with Norman. One day Marie, Norman's next-door neighbor, stopped me and said Norman seemed to be growing crippled, so she had made an appointment for him with a foot doctor. "Would you mind driving Norman to the doctor's office?" she asked.

The podiatrist, Dr. McKemie, looked over Norman's feet and then took me aside. Norman's feet had been deformed, he said, by wearing shoes that were too small for too many years of his life. He also asked me whether Norman ever washed his feet—the doctor was obviously having trouble keeping his lunch down.

Turning back to work on his patient, Dr. McKemie removed the nails from each toe. Norman hardly flinched; the nails had been dead a long time. Taking a surgical knife, the doctor next carved out what looked like a plastic cone—a hard callus—from the ball of each foot. Then he packed the surgical wounds with sulfur and salve and bandaged them. He instructed Norman to bathe his feet as often as possible and soak them in a pail at night. I couldn't get Norman to wash at that time, but I did buy him a plastic pail in which he would soak his feet when I visited him every evening.

Norman and I went back to see the foot doctor several times as his feet healed from the minor surgery. After one such trip, we stopped off at a nearby shopping mall. Norman had never been to one. (He had lived for many years within a world that was not much larger than four or five square blocks.) He had never been on an escalator, either. Hesitant before getting on, he was nearly unsettled as the ground under his feet moved. As we approached the top, I could see that he was wondering how to get off.

Quickly, I climbed the few remaining stairs and hopped off, then turned to face Norman. "Jump," I said. "Hop off, Norman. Now!"

He took what was for him a sizable

standing jump, landed heavily on his still-healing feet, and stabilized, like an elderly gymnast recovering from an awkward dismount. He reared his head back in that way he has and gave his grin.

Norman was so like a child at these times, discovering something new. The pleasure of being with him was the pleasure of rediscovering the familiar, learning again to be amazed at an escalator, a TV program, a lawnmower that's finally running right.

At the mall, as well as at the ball game, Norman was fascinated with the people. I was constantly struck by how open he was to others after a lifetime of neglect. He was so trusting.

Norman also had an unusual capacity to be absorbed in the scene before him—to really *see* everything. I'm sure the stores' window dressers would have liked everyone to be as attentive to how they had cocked the braceleted wrist of one mannequin and placed a broad-brimmed hat on another. Norman was alive to the whole scene, and being with him sharpened my perceptions as well.

Chapter
11

SPLISH, SPLASH

"'Norman' I asked, 'have you ever been clean?'"
"'It's been years,' he answered. 'I'm a hermit, you know.'"

After our last trip to the foot doctor, I didn't see Norman for a while. I finally went back over to his house one day, carrying a brown suit that I had decided I wouldn't wear anymore. It had a couple of shiny spots on it and wasn't particularly in style any longer, but it certainly seemed good enough for old Norman.

As I walked across the street, I made sure I held the suit high enough for the neighbors to see. After Norman let me in and I told him what I had, he directed me to his bedroom closet. I pulled the string to turn the light on and saw racks of clothes, all of them obviously castoffs of other well-meaning people. There were ties of all kinds—bolo ties, ties that seemed to sparkle, wide ones, and skinny ones—nothing that anybody would want to wear. And on the floor was a whole row of old shoes of every description, probably few that actually fit.

A voice spoke to me, "Love your neighbor as yourself."

I began to pray, "God, if You'll give me some money somehow, I'll buy Norman a suit that costs more than any suit I've ever bought for myself."

It wasn't long thereafter that my Methodist neighbor asked me to fill in and provide the music for an upcoming revival. Fill in? I felt a little insulted, but then I decided that's what we're supposed to do: fill in. Surprisingly, a gracious offering was collected at the end of the revival and given to me. That got me excited, because I knew instantly that this money was for Norman. We went downtown to the best men's store. An impeccably dressed, nice young man waited on us. He took Norman to the suit rack, and Norman selected his suit himself. It was a tasteful, navy dress suit, with fancy stitching at the lapels. I also bought him a shirt, new socks, and new shoes. I realized that I really *hadn't* ever spent that much money on clothes for myself.

After I had driven him home, I asked Norman if he would like to go to the gospel singing service at a church that night.

"You'd be my guest," I said. "You could wear your new suit."

"I like music," he said. "Let's go."

"But Norman," I continued, "have you ever been clean?"

"It's been years," he answered. "I'm a hermit, you know."

"Well, there's one thing you have to do."

He looked at me, questioning.

"We're pretty good buddies, Norman, right?"

"Yeah, Mike, we're pretty good buddies."

"Well then, today is your day, Norman."

"Today?" he responded, thoroughly confused.

"Yep, today is the day, Norman. Today is the day you take a bath." Later, as I helped him get ready, I asked, "Why don't you take baths regularly?"

He said something that, once again, I'll never forget: "Because I figured, who'd care?"

Then he told me more about his hermit-like life. His dad had been killed in the coal mines when Norman was a little boy. His father had just gone to work one day and never come home. Norman remembered some men coming to his house to tell his mother and him that the roof of the mine had fallen in. He also remembered his dad's funeral. Norman's uncle was there, but he hadn't seen him since. He told me again how much he missed his mother. For a decade he had made do on his own. He ended his story by repeating, "Who'd care if I take a bath?"

"Well, Norman, I care," I said. "You don't want to get ring around the collar on that new shirt, do you? Let's get you really clean."

I went to the grocery store and bought a bar of Lava soap, a big sponge, and SOS pads. I cleaned out his tub. I threw away all the paper sacks he had put back after the Methodist ladies left. Next I put the rubber stopper in the bottom of the tub and tried to turn on the hot water faucet—it fell into the tub.

So I went across the street to my house, got some tools, and fixed it. It leaked, but it worked.

Slowly the tub began to fill with water. I rinsed it, refilled it with warm water, and told Norman to go into the bedroom and take his clothes off. "Norman," I said, "here's the plan. You get in the tub while I wait in your living room. And when you're clean, you holler for me, and I'll come and see if you really are."

Soon I heard Norman humming in the tub. It sounded as though he was enjoying himself. Finally he called out, "OK, I'm clean."

I went in there, pulled the curtain back, and looked at him. I couldn't believe my eyes! It looked as if he'd just smeared mud on himself. A pig wallowing in a mud puddle to keep cool on a hot summer day would have felt right at home with him. I shook my head slowly and said, "Norman, I don't think you understand what I'm talking about here. I'm saying you need to be *clean*. Give me your head, Norman."

He bent over, and I got a gentle headlock on him. I took that Lava soap and that sponge, and I began to scrub his head. "Mmm, mmm," he said, sounding like a boy whose mother was washing behind his long-neglected ears.

Suddenly I spied a little bit of white hair! Before long, all his hair was a beautiful white instead of dull gray. After his hair and scalp, I scrubbed his face, his ears, and his neck. Then I handed him the sponge and soap and said, "Listen, big boy, from there on down belongs to you! Get it clean!"

I returned to the living room, and then it was back to the bathroom when Norman announced he was clean.

"Not good enough, Norman," I said after looking him over. "Try again."

We repeated this process maybe a half-dozen times. Finally he was finished, but not without water all over the walls, the floor—everywhere. You could rub your thumb anyplace on his body, though, and he was squeaky clean!

I bought him a new toothbrush and

toothpaste, too, and he brushed those four teeth over and over. I shaved the whiskers off his clean face. We washed his glasses, styled his hair, got his new clothes on, and tied his tie.

When we were done, I stepped back to look at the finished product and concluded that it looked as if I would be escorting a state senator to the gospel sing that evening! Actually, Norman sometimes reminded me of my own father when he was dressed up. They were strangely similar.

We arrived dramatically late for the program. And I have to confess a bit of meanness in me. I got a lot of enjoyment from those folks who walked up to me and said, "Welcome, Mike. Who's your friend?"

When they reached over and took his hand to shake it, at that very moment I'd say, "This is Norman." I thoroughly enjoyed watching their reactions.

After the service, I asked Norman if he would like to go over and check out the new Hardee's restaurant on the edge of town. Proudly drawing himself up to his full height, he asked, "Do you think they'll notice my new suit?"

Chapter 12

AN
UNFORGETTABLE
VACATION

*"The Lord seemed to say to
me, 'You see, this is what's
been happening to Norman
all his life. People have
victimized him. No wonder
he's afraid of other people.'"*

It had been a busy, busy year. I had been working at the coal mine during the week and singing in churches on the weekends. I wasn't sure whether it was a coincidence, but as my involvement with Norman increased, so did my opportunities to serve the Lord with my music.

One day that summer, as I was out in the yard working on that tree stump again, I was telling the Lord how tired I was and how much I was looking forward to my vacation. The Lord seemed to say, "Your vacation. That's great. Look over there at Norman's house. Wonder how long it's been since he had a vacation? Maybe he never has had a vacation. Maybe you should take him with you."

I thought, "That can't be the Lord saying that, because He knows we're going to Opryland! What would Norman do at an amusement park?"

A couple of weeks later, we drove down to Nashville, my wife and girls in the back seat, Norman sitting over where Carmel usually sits. She and the girls were glad to have "Uncle Norman" along. They got the same kick I did out of watching him experience things for the first time. I noticed, too, that he was beginning to be more relaxed around people, and he didn't talk to himself as much as he had before.

We bought him a new shirt for the occasion, and we got him a room next to ours at the hotel. Showing him the room, I turned on the TV and opened the door to the bathroom. "This is how you turn the shower on, Norman," I said. "You can take a shower, or you can take a bath. You're going to be in here all alone, so you can soak in the tub for hours if you want to."

When I got back to our room, I heard the water running, which gave me hope. But the next morning, when we picked him up for Opryland, I could see that he hadn't been in the bathtub.

As we went into Opryland, I thought about what rides Norman would like. He was about sixty-two years old then (1975), and I was afraid he might have a heart condition, so we steered clear of the Wabash Cannonball!

However, I thought he could handle the bumper cars. I asked him if he had ever been in one. He hadn't. I told him to get in, push the pedal, turn the wheel, and have a good time.

Norman sat in his bumper car, his chin lifted, grinning, looking at all the girlfriends who wanted to hit their boyfriends and all the mothers who wanted to ram the fathers.

The ride started, and before anyone knew it, Norman had the whole crowd of bumper cars pinned to one side! I don't know how it could have happened like that. But he had his car sideways and had jammed everyone into a corner.

The others got mad. The time of the ride was going by after they'd stood in line for quite a while, and now they couldn't move. They yelled for Norman to get out of the way. He was looking around, confused, and saying, "Heh." He looked to me and said, "Heh" again. He couldn't figure out what was going on or how to operate the car.

We all thought it was funny at first. "Carmel, look," I said, "he's got everyone caught over there." We started to laugh, along with the girls and other spectators nearby.

Finally, somebody got loose. And that person circled all the way around the rink and *boom,* slammed into Norman. That freed the logjam. Then, one by one, the others came around and rammed into Norman, laughing all the while.

He tried to get out of the way, but he had no control of the car, and they were coming at him from all sides anyway. He went, "Oh, oh," and started to panic. Giving up his efforts to control the car, he started to climb out. I didn't know for sure, but I was afraid he might be electrocuted if he walked on that rink. Sparks showered down from the electrical ceiling.

I called out to the operator to stop the ride, but no one could hear me, not with the music playing. Thank the Lord, the time ran out before Norman could get out of the car. I hurried over to him. He was trembling.

Norman never complained or said anything, but he looked at me, his eyes magnified by his glasses, and his look seemed to say, "I trusted you. I don't understand why you would do that to me."

I thought about how I had been trying to establish a relationship with him all this time, and I felt I had betrayed him. Then the Lord seemed to say to me, "You see, this is what's been happening to Norman all his life. People have victimized him. No wonder he's afraid of other people. No wonder he tries to scare people off sometimes."

I thought of the kids who poked him and the high-school students who threw snowballs at him. I thought of people bringing him old, junky clothes they wouldn't wear. (Later in our relationship, others would victimize Norman as well: a group of junior high kids broke into his house and then had the nerve to come back a second time.)

Norman and I sat on a bench together, and I tried to explain how I thought he would be able to steer the car. We had a snack, and I watched over him until he calmed down.

The rest of the trip proved uneventful, and I think Norman enjoyed his time, with the exception of the bumper car ride. But the incident made me think about how people—even people in the church—victimize one another as well: the boss lording it over his employee, the soloist looking down her nose at the other choir members. Why is there so much meanness in us?

NORMAN'S NEW BIRTH

"As I searched Norman's face, I could tell he was having a hard time understanding. I was desperate that he see the truth."

One bright and clear Sunday when we came home from church, about two years after I first met Norman, I knew somehow that it was his day again—not for a physical bath, but for a spiritual one. I had noticed a Bible out on the lampstand by Norman's bed, and I thought he had been reading it.

Still, I was worried about how I would convey to him his need for the Lord. What would I say? I asked a local pastor who had the reputation of being particularly good with people to come with me. I thought he might be able to help when words failed me. Ever since my first real discussion with Norman at the Dairy Queen, I had known he had given "serious consideration" to becoming a Christian. But since that time he hadn't opened his thoughts on the subject to me again. It was as if his views on the matter were as dark and hidden as the interior of his house had once been.

We knocked on Norman's door that afternoon, and he invited us in. As we opened the Bible, I wondered where we should start. The pastor, who was more experienced in witnessing, explained from the book of Romans that even though Norman was a good person compared to some, he still needed to invite Jesus into his heart.

This struck me, because over the last two years I had come to consider Norman one of the best people, if not *the* best person, I knew. I already thought of him as one of God's favorites. Norman was rarely angry with anyone. He didn't think more highly of himself than he should; he hardly had any expectations at all. I had talked to Norman originally thinking of what I wanted to share with him. But in just letting me get to know him, he had shared so much more with me.

How could I explain God's love to him? How could I tell him how much God wanted to give Himself to him? God longed to be his friend—to talk with him, to be there for him through the lonely hours of the night. God wanted to be an everlasting day for

Norman, dispelling all the darkness of sadness, neglect, and abuse.

"You *are* a good man, Norman," I said. "I know that about you. Yet even a good man like you still needs to ask Jesus to come into his heart. It's as if Jesus stands at the door and knocks, but you must come to that door and invite Him in. He wants to be your friend, Norman. He wants to do for you what you can't do for yourself."

The pastor tried to summarize the plan of salvation from the Bible. He explained that because of the sin of Adam and Eve, we were all separated from God, but that God through Jesus Christ had provided a way for us to be reunited.

As I searched Norman's face, I could tell he was having a hard time understanding. I was desperate that he see the truth. I thought of the two years we had been friends. I had done one thing or another for Norman, but that was nothing compared to what God wanted to do for him. How could I tell him? "Please, God," I prayed, "let Norman understand. I don't know how to explain it to him. You just have to be there for him."

All of a sudden, Norman's clouded expression grew clear. He said, "I—I know what you're sayin'. Like—like my windows there, bein' so dirty." His voice was gruff as always, but a tenderness made it as friendly as an old, woolly dog. "Wouldn't do much good to just clean the outside of 'em. I'd have to clean the inside, too."

He looked over at his living room windows. I remembered the day my Methodist friends and I had washed them, the light flooding through for the first time in many years. I knew we had done our most important witnessing that day. At the Spirit's inspiration, care for his home had provided a picture of what he had to do to care for his soul. "In my house are many mansions," the Lord said. We're all taught to understand our spiritual welfare through the things of this world.

"Norman," I said, "you need to pray for Jesus to come into your life, because the Bible says every single one of us must confess out of our own mouth—not being ashamed of Him—that He died at Calvary for our sins."

We bowed our heads real quick, and it was quiet. I didn't know whether Norman would pray or not. I thought of saying a prayer he could repeat after me. But then, on his own, he said, "Well, God, I want to ask You to come into Norman's heart and be my Savior, because that's what the preachers used to say on the radio on Sunday morning. My mama used to listen to them. And that's what that Bible over there says that I've been reading for myself. And so, come into my heart. Come into Norman's heart and be my Savior. Amen."

He looked up at me. "Did I do OK?" he asked.

Tears came to my eyes. I looked at the pastor, and he had tears in *his* eyes. Neither one of us could speak, yet we wanted to let Norman know that the angels in heaven were rejoicing. I could hear those heavenly hosts shouting hallelujah and raising all kinds of glory. "You did just fine, Norman," I choked out finally. "Just fine."

LEARNING TO LOVE

"The Lord's plan for me looked like a combination of the wearisome and the tedious. I guess I wondered whether the Lord Himself didn't have too low an opinion of me."

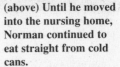

(above) Until he moved into the nursing home, Norman continued to eat straight from cold cans.

(left) A photo of young Norman, with his high school diploma alongside.

(above) Norman and
Mike talk in a photo
taken in about 1980.

(right) One of
Norman's favorite
activities today is tak-
ing in a Cardinals'
baseball game.

(left) West Frankfort coal miners head for home after their shift underground.

(below) Norman tries to start a lawnmower similar to the one Mike offered to help him with at the beginning of their friendship.

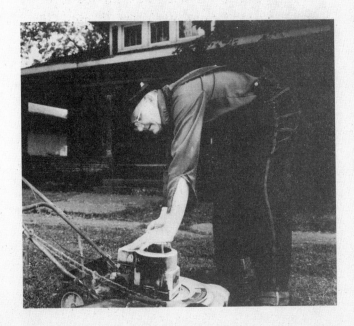

(top) The kitchen in Norman's house, much as it appeared when Mike first saw it.

(bottom) Norman's living room–clean windows, but he never stopped collecting!

(above) Mike, Norman, and the rest of the film crew took time out for this group picture on the front porch of Norman's house.

(left) Part of becoming a film star was getting made up for the cam-era—a process Norman really enjoyed.

In this photo from about 1980, Norman stands with shovel and bucket in front of his coal bin. Fortunately, he no longer has to worry about feeding a furnace.

was lying on his back, I would elevate the knee with one hand and gently pump and rotate his ankle with the other. This was painful for Norman, to put it mildly. He would yell as if I were twisting his leg off!

During the time he was bedfast, I kept a water pitcher and a glass by his bedside, and I tended his chamber pot. I also fixed his furnace, an old-fashioned coal burner that needed constant attention. I couldn't seem to keep from burning my hand on the hot ashes as I carried the pan out to the coal bin.

My lowest moments in my friendship with Norman may have come on those cold nights, tending that balky furnace. Although I had seen a wonderful change in Norman, my efforts with him weren't fun anymore. I had long since realized there would be no applause in this for me.

When I would go out in the alley, my fingers singed from the hot coal ashes, wading in the snow and rain out to the bin, and then creep over to the shed where Norman stored his coal—the roof of the enclosure so low that I always seemed to bump my head as I shoveled fresh coal into the bucket—I would look up at the night sky and wonder whether God even cared about my efforts. I wanted to serve Him with my music, and I felt deeply resentful that this was the task He had given me instead.

In a way, the God-shaped void we talk

about when we describe our yearning for God is like the desire for applause, for acceptance and love. Yet God doesn't fill that void the way the recognition of others seems to. This was a hard lesson for me to learn.

When I felt resentful, a lot of other thoughts crept in as well. The renovation of Norman's house was an ongoing task. I didn't have a lot of money in those days, and sometimes I was hard-pressed to buy a gallon of paint. I wondered whether I was doing right by my family in spending so much of my time and money on Norman. Carmel and the girls didn't seem to mind, but why was he my job?

My father had taught us kids to be self-reliant. He earned a hard living from the mines for our family of eleven, and he always kept us fed. He taught us the value of hard work, and he sure believed charity began at home.

I had suffered in the past by not taking my father's advice, by ignoring his common sense. I had profited by obeying him.

When my secular singing career collapsed, for example, my father helped me get a job in the mines. Carmel and I were married by then, and we were starving. My only job was racking balls in a pool hall for less than minimum wage. My father sent me to the man who did the hiring in the mines, and because of my father's reputation as a hard worker, I'm sure, he hired me.

I had dreaded going into the mines. If I weren't literally buried alive there, I was sure my singing career would at least be suffocated. My hopes and ambitions would die as certainly as coal dust produces black lung.

Yet I had done the right thing. I had gone to work to support my family, and I eventually became an inspector of mines, a respected position in the community and a fairly safe one. I had never gotten anywhere following my own instincts. In fact, at moments in my life I had courted serious trouble following my own instincts—like when I took on the obligations of marriage without a proper job. Singing in some of the grungiest dives around the country was another example. I felt I had lived down a lot of my past mistakes, and I had done so, mainly, by heeding my father's counsel.

But I had another Father, a heavenly one. I had been led to study Proverbs, and the verses that came to me over and over were: "Trust in the LORD with all thine heart; and lean not unto thine own understanding. In all thy ways acknowledge him, and he shall direct thy paths" (3:5-6).

I felt I was acknowledging Him in my "ways," and I just had to trust that He would see to my future. In the cold of those dark Illinois nights, however, there didn't seem to be much of a future for me. Even if I was being the Lord's servant, I was doing work *anybody* could have done. The Lord's plan for me looked like a combination of the wearisome and the tedious. I guess I wondered whether the Lord Himself didn't have too low an opinion of me.

But then Norman and I started to see positive results. He improved slowly. In time he was walking with the use of crutches, and then a cane. I was supposed to encourage him to walk. The layout of his house allowed him to make a circuit from the kitchen through the hallway and into his bedroom, the living room, and back into the kitchen. After several go-rounds, he would want to quit. I challenged him to extend his walking time, to do a little more every day. Gradually, he was regaining the spring in his step.

One night as I was about to leave Norman's house, the Lord impressed upon me, "Before you leave Norman each night, before you turn out his lights and put the lock on the door, have him pray with you."

The first night we tried it, I did all the praying. Norman was a Christian now, and he was reading the materials I gave him about his new faith. He seemed to like my praying with him.

Then one night I said, "Norman, you pray." We were in his bedroom. I remember hearing the old clock on the mantel ticking, the wind whistling through the cracks of the house, the boards creaking and groaning. Would he say anything? The time passed slowly.

Finally he said, "Well, God, I just want to thank You for Mike, because I don't know what I would have done without him. Amen."

I left and went across the yard to my house, and I started to realize that night that if you're going to love somebody, you really need to love him for his own sake and not in expectation of some reward or pat on the back.

When I closed my front door, I found my Bible and read from 1 Corinthians 13: "Though I speak with the tongues of men and of angels, and have not charity [love], I am become as sounding brass, or a tinkling cymbal." Then I read where it said, "Though I . . . understand all mysteries, and all knowledge; and though I have all faith, . . . and have not charity, I am nothing" (verses 1-2).

So I kept going over to Norman's. One night I got him out of the tub and gave him his pajamas—just the tops (they were so long they reached down to his knees). I *forgot* to give him his undershorts. I turned the lights out and said good-bye to him, then locked the door behind me. As I started away from his house, I remembered I had forgotten to pray with him.

I unlocked the door, went in, turned the light back on, walked to his bedside, and said, "Norman, I forgot something. You know what I forgot, don't you?" I meant our prayers.

He said, "Yeah, you forgot my shorts!"

We laughed together about that.

I gave him his underclothes, turned my back while he put them on, and then got him in bed again. "I meant I forgot to pray," I said.

Finally we said our prayers that night, and we did it each night for weeks until he got back into the swing of things.

One day the next year, in the wintertime again, I got a phone call from the neighborhood grocery store. The folks there had been kind to Norman for years, letting him buy his food on credit. As I've said, another neighbor, Marie, helped Norman with his accounts, including his bill at the grocery. She wrote most of his checks and generally supervised his business dealings. Norman would have been institutionalized soon after his mother died, I'm sure, without her help.

But now the man from the store said, "We love Norman, Mike. Don't misunderstand. And we don't want to offend him, but the truth is, he *stinks*. My other customers are complaining openly. I've got to ask you, much as I hate to do it, to tell him not to come in here anymore."

I was shocked. I thought he was bathing much more than he had previously. He looked cleaner when I saw him come and go from his house. I didn't know what to think. My first response was to get angry with the people at the grocery store.

A few days later, however, the man from the Dairy Queen called. "Mike," he said, "I've got to ask you to tell Norman not to come in here anymore. He stinks so bad he's running my other customers off."

Then I became angry with Norman. I had seen him become a Christian, but I thought he was making a mockery of that experience by not cleaning himself up physically, by continuing to live as if no one cared about him—not even God.

I still had a lot of pent-up resentment in me, too, I must admit. Those many nights of trudging across to his house in the snow, burning my fingers on the ashes, taking care of him like a baby, bending the damaged knee, helping him walk again, and doing all the rest—was it all for nothing? Had Norman not really changed for the better?

I stomped over to his house, charged in his back door, and made him sit down at the kitchen table. "Don't say a word to me," I told him. "I'm going to do the talking. I'm getting calls from these businesses. The grocery store called me. The Dairy Queen called me. They said you stink when you go in their place, and they won't let you in there anymore. You can't go back. And I want you to know you've embarrassed me. You've embarrassed yourself. You're supposed to be a Christian, and you stink."

He tried to interrupt me.

"Don't say anything!" I insisted. "This time I'm not going to sit and listen to you mumble. I'm going to talk to you. And here's what I've got to say. I'm through with you! I've worked with you, I've scrubbed your floors, I've carried your coal, carried your slopjar and everything else, and I'm not messing with you anymore. And I want you to know something. This is the last time I'll ever be in your house."

Harsh as it sounds, I meant every word. I was furious. "I'm going to tell you just one more thing, big boy," I continued. "At least I'm going to have the satisfaction of knowing, before I leave, that the last time I laid eyes on you—and this will be the last time—you were clean. So march in there. Get your clothes off, and get in that tub. I'm going to leave your house this final time with you in the tub getting clean. Don't argue with me."

Norman got up like a little child and went in the bedroom. I sat in the kitchen so I could see him go through the hallway into the bathroom. I wanted to make sure he didn't con me. I had convinced myself, since getting those calls, that he must be nothing but a con artist, using me to do all his work for him and not really changing.

He came out of his bedroom and into the hall. All he had on were his shorts. Suddenly, I saw his leg. It was swollen almost double its normal size! "Norman," I said, "come here."

He hobbled into the kitchen. When he turned to one side, I could see that his calf had an abscess in it the size of a grapefruit. It looked as if a rat had eaten away at the leg; the wound was green and running. The stench was unbearable. I had never seen gangrene before, but I knew this had to be it.

I had Norman sit down, and I ran next door, where a state policeman was visiting. He came back with me to look at the wound, and he told me we had to get Norman to the hospital right away. "That's gangrene," he confirmed. "His leg's rotting off his body." Privately, he told me he hoped the leg would not have to be amputated.

The amazing thing to me was that Norman had never complained, had never come to my house and shown me the swelling and infection. I think he was so used to misery that he resigned himself to anything that came his way.

How I felt would be hard to describe— like the scum of the earth.

I took Norman to the hospital in my car. As we drove, I heard him chuckling to himself quietly. I hadn't said a word yet, because I was trying to come up with the right thing to say and because I was so embarrassed. His chuckling broke the ice. "Why are you laughing?" I asked.

"Boy, you sure were mad," he said. "You were beating on my kitchen table and everything."

That's Norman. He just laughed about it all. And he was still my friend.

It turned out that Norman had cut himself using the pail I bought for him to soak his feet in. (The plastic had a sharp edge to it where the handle hooked on.) The superficial wound this caused had never healed, because in damaging his knee, the circulation in his leg deteriorated, weakening the limb's recuperative powers.

Norman almost did lose his leg. He went through surgery and another long period of recuperation. Now, years later, the last word we've had is that the leg has improved just slightly; it's edged back toward health and away from the need to be amputated. It still swells and must be constantly bandaged— the wound has a crust over it. Norman just lives with these problems, never complaining, thankful for whatever help he's given. He has a quiet courage that I've learned to admire over the years.

Chapter 16

GANGRENE OF
THE SOUL

*"I hadn't felt such
humiliation in many years.
And I was surprised that
having been a dedicated
Christian the past seven
years, I could still
sink that low."*

Norman forgave me quickly for blowing up at him, but I had a hard time forgiving myself. The incident caused me to do some serious soul-searching.

I hadn't felt such humiliation in many years. And I was surprised that having been a dedicated Christian the past seven years, I could still sink that low. I saw in this crisis, though, a chance to reexamine episodes from my past that had caused me the same kind of pain.

When I became a Christian, I never told anyone about the darkest of the events that led to my conversion. I was only now examining those things for the first time myself.

I had gone into the mines with the awful

feeling that my dream of becoming a singer was at an end. Yet I nurtured that dream for the next five or six years as best I could.

For example, before I became a Christian, I sang on the weekends in nightclubs. I was married and thought I should be more settled down. I also felt guilty about hanging out in bars. But that was the only way I could see to keep my voice going and my dreams alive. At the same time, I began to drink screwdrivers (vodka and orange juice) to dull my conscience.

Two nights from that period stand out in my memory. In one, an old rock 'n' roll singer who was on a downhill slide played a local club. Actually, he sang very little that night. Mostly he sat at the bar and drank. He kicked off his band's set, sang a couple of songs, and then turned his responsibilities over to the rest of the band while he watched and boozed. (He tried to make it seem as though he were giving the younger fellows a showcase.)

His guitar player found out that I sang sometimes at the club, and he asked me to sit in. I sang "It's Only Make-Believe," a Conway Twitty song. I was hitting the high notes that night, and the band sounded great behind me.

Maybe too great. The fading star didn't like being upstaged. He came over and grabbed the microphone in the middle of the song. Angry and drunk, he tried to sing the last couple of verses.

He was so drunk that he forgot one crucial fact: he was a baritone. His veins stood out as he tried to hit the high notes and failed. The people laughed at him.

For a moment there I felt proud that I had won this impromptu singing competition with a star. Then, as I took another drink from my screwdriver and realized I was hardly getting set to go on to bigger and better things, I saw myself in that pathetic guy. I might soon be a drunk staggering onto a stage somewhere, grabbing a microphone and making a fool of myself, and all this without ever having achieved the fame this man had once known.

That didn't stop my drinking, though. And in the second sadly memorable night, just before Christmas, I led the whole bar— so they tell me—in a round of carols. I must have been in a blackout, because I don't remember anything about it. I would never have done something so blasphemous without being dead drunk. That was the first and last time I was ever really drunk. It discouraged me like you couldn't believe. "What a person I am!" I told myself.

That bewildered feeling—what a person I am!—who really am I?—what am I capable of?—that balled-up emotion came back to me after reading Norman out for an affliction that he was innocently and helplessly suffering. I was especially troubled because I hadn't been a Christian when I had made those past mistakes, but now I was. Yet I still suffered from the same kind of pride.

I began to realize that my pride, my gangrene of the soul, was a condition that I nurtured as much as made war against. Reflecting on these things, I started to think of my pride as a wound and my relationship with Norman as the salve for that wound. And it seemed to me that for that salve to have the power to heal me, I would have to keep it hidden under a bandage of silence. I resolved not to tell *anyone anything anymore* about my friendship with Norman.

I also rededicated myself to helping Norman as the abscess healed, undertaking another round of caring for him at home. Finding it hard to keep up with his balky furnace, which often went out at night, I finally took a good look at it to see whether its performance might be improved.

When I had first entered the house, I noticed that the air was always full of soot. The curtains rained dust, and everything you touched was dusty. After I painted the walls, they were no more than dry when they were dusty once more.

All this led me to conclude that the furnace couldn't possibly be breathing properly, so I made arrangements for the chimney to be checked. But before the chimney sweep came over, I personally checked the flue pipe, the aluminum cylinder that ran from the furnace into the chimney. I forgot, however, that you have to handle the flue pipe with extreme caution. When I tried to dislodge it, it swung loose from the wall and covered me with soot. I looked as if I'd walked a hundred miles through the Mojave Desert in a dust storm!

The flue pipe had to be replaced. (We hadn't had that type of furnace in our house in a long time, and I had forgotten the trouble those flue pipes caused.) It proved to be the main problem. The chimney was partially blocked as well, and we cleaned that out, too.

Those measures still didn't solve the problem entirely, however. The mechanism that fed the coal into the furnace was in such bad shape that I finally decided to buy a much better unit for Norman, one that was more automatic and had to be tended only once a day.

With Norman's abscess, it wasn't a good idea for him to soak in the still water of a bathtub, so Carmel and I also decided to put in a shower for him. That was one of the last repairs we undertook in the house. And then I had the idea that Norman might like a small, wood-burning stove in his bedroom—something to make the place more cheery.

By taking these actions, I worked out of my despondent mood. Even if my helping Norman was motivated partially by guilt rather than feelings of love, I was helping him. I knew from the Scriptures that the real test of love is acting for someone's good regardless of your feelings. And I wasn't looking for recognition any longer; I was concentrating on what was good for Norman.

to the toilet. It was just sitting there in a plastic bag, with the instructions inside, leaning up against the wall.

On one particular visit to Norman's house, I became convicted, absolutely convicted, that the Lord wanted me to repair Norman's toilet. Still I resisted—for three days. On the last night, Carmel and I were sitting in our living room, watching television. I hadn't asked her for advice about the toilet, because she was always quick to say I ought to do that kind of thing, and that was the last counsel I wanted to hear this time. She didn't know anything about what was on my mind.

All of a sudden I turned around and out of the clear blue said, "I'm not going to do it!" Carmel looked up from paging through the Sears catalogue and gave me a look that said, "So, the Lord's after you again. Whatever it is, you'd better get on with it." She knows me pretty well.

I couldn't stand it. Late that night, making sure the neighbors would be asleep, I put my coveralls on, put my collar up, sheathed my hands with work gloves, grabbed my toolbox, and stole across the street to Norman's. (Laughing about it later, I've often said I would have worn a surgeon's mask if I had owned one.)

When Norman let me in, a little surprised to see me so late, I said, "I'm going to

work on your house some, Norman." He
went into the living room to sit in his rocker
and wait.

I went into the bathroom, opened the
toolbox, and set it near the door. I tried to
gauge with my eye what size wrench would
fit the one nut left on the one bolt that was
still in place. I couldn't see up under the
stool very well, though, and I was trying to
proceed gingerly, not wanting to get too
close. As I tried to clamp the wrench on at
arm's length, I couldn't find a wrench that
would hold. I realized then that the nut and
bolt were probably heavily corroded.

In desperation, I finally lay on the floor
and slid up underneath the stool, directly
under the bolt. My cheek brushed the cold
porcelain. I found out the truth of what
someone told me later: you have to hug
those things to work on them.

I twisted and twisted, and finally the nut
gave way. All that rust and corrosion *fell
right in my eye.*

That got to me. I had one major pity
party for Mike Adkins right there and then.
God had given me all kinds of singing and
entertaining gifts, I felt, and here He had me
playing to a toilet stool—one that spit in my
eye! I had to be crazy. None of this meant
anything. No one cared. I was so tired of this
I could've screamed!

I finished the job, though.

In spite of all I had done to fix up Norman's house, I stubbornly resisted tackling one last repair job. I had reached the point in my own heart where I had finished everything I thought God should require of me. And I had, indeed, gained a new degree of maturity through the experience of helping Norman. I wasn't looking for an out anymore. I wasn't thinking to myself, "Now that's done, and I don't have to worry about Norman ever again." I knew that as long as we lived in our home, he would be a neighbor, and he'd always be a friend for whose care I would share responsibility. I was really living *with* him now, in the day to day, coping with new problems as they came up. But there was this one thing I wouldn't do.

In addition to the types of help I've already mentioned, Carmel and I replenished his pantry with foodstuffs, bought a new bed for him, sorted and ordered the junk he had accumulated over the years (pencils, buttons, paper clips, and rubber bands, to name a few), and rebuilt the closet in his bedroom. I also took him to the eye doctor and got him a new pair of glasses. Still, there was one thing I *would not do.*

His bathroom had been almost entirely redone. I had fixed his bathtub and sink, repapered the walls, put in a new ceiling, and was installing a new light fixture. But the thing I could not bring myself to work on was the stool. I kept thinking, "Well, there's a limit. Isn't there a limit? There *ought* to be a limit." I sang in churches; I was a deacon in my own church; I wore a pin-striped suit on Sundays. I had my *dignity.* There was a limit.

Yet every time I looked at that stool, the Lord told me to fix it. Sometimes in working in the bathroom, I would knock up against it and cause the lid and ring to flop to one side. Only one bolt held it in place; the other had long since disappeared. But I fought and fought against the idea of working on it.

Someone—I don't know who to this day—had put a new lid and ring right next

Chapter
17

ANYTHING
BUT THAT!

"I kept thinking, 'Well, there's a limit. Isn't there a limit? There ought to be a limit.'"

As I was walking home, a Scripture came to me: "Inasmuch as ye have done it unto one of the least of these my brethren, ye have done it unto me" (Matt. 25:40). That night I sensed something changed in me. I knew that I had been right—that I ought not to mention this experience to anyone. For I was learning that only one audience mattered, only one person's opinion, and that was the Lord Himself. It seemed as if He had to get me away from everyone else to direct my attention to Him alone.

There isn't any limit to God's love. And there's no limit to His mercy, either. He could only have taught me what He did that night in a place of obscurity, a place, like the Bethlehem manger, where He so often chooses to be born.

from holiness. When we're seeking God first, those things can have their proper place. But if we make them substitutes for God Himself, they function as idols, and God, in His mercy, can't allow us to have anything to do with them.

I had made my career my idol for so long that I was extremely distrustful of what seemed to be God's permission to return to it. Even after I had written those ten songs, I hesitated to record an album. I wanted to make sure God was in everything I did from then on.

With that in mind, I asked David Ingalls, a Christian singer who was touring through our part of the country, about making the album. He told me, "You should have already recorded your songs. That's how soon God wants you to make that album."

Receiving this and other indications that I should go ahead, I borrowed the money from the bank. I remember getting the payment book, with its thirty-six stubs, and thinking that if I was wrong, I could still repay the money out of my regular earnings as a mine inspector.

Through a disc jockey friend of mine, I found out about a recording studio in South Carolina called The Sounding Board (it has moved since to Nashville), and I felt tremendously confirmed in what I was doing because the people there were like-minded.

So in the fall of 1978, I recorded my first
Christian album. Soon the albums, in both
LPs and eight-track cassettes, arrived at our
home.

We had some confirmation fairly soon
that what we were doing was right. I had
begun singing in area churches some time
before. After the albums arrived, the first
church I went to, I sensed that God didn't
want me to promote the album at all. Like
the first time I felt prompted to cross the
street and help Norman, I couldn't believe
right away that this was God's leading.

Looking back, I realize I was thinking
more of the payment book than of God's
will at that point, but God overcame my
resistance by giving me a sense of reassur-
ance that He would be a better salesman for
the album than I could ever be.

So at that church that day, I stayed at the
altar and prayed with people instead of
going back to the book table to sell the
album. I felt as though the Lord was saying,
"Prefer others," and that's what I tried to do.
A friend of mine, Dennis Amsden, came up
to me after the service and said, "While you
were praying with people, I felt I should go
back there and stand by your records and
tapes. I hope you don't mind. I sold a ton of
them for you."

I went to the bank the next day and made
three payments instead of the one that was

backing out of my driveway in my old, yel-
low 1970 Pontiac on my way uptown to pay
my electric bill. I thought the bill was too
high, and I was rehearsing in my mind what
I was going to say when I reached the col-
lection office. In the midst of my irritable
thoughts, these words came to me:

> What's wrong with My children,
>   why won't they praise Me?
> Am I not the King of kings?
> Am I not the Lord of lords?
> What's wrong with My children,
>   why won't they praise Me?
> I've given them everything,
>   yet they have no joy.

I knew the truth of that, and I knew that the
words had come somehow from God, that
He had given me an entire song.

I pulled back into my driveway, went
inside and fetched the Autoharp, sat down,
composed the melody, and then wrote
down the lyrics with the chord changes.
And in the next few months, God gave me
ten songs altogether.

God so often gives us what we want after
we put Him first: "Seek ye first the kingdom
of God . . . and all these things shall be
added unto you." It seems to me our mate-
rial desires often aren't so much wrong in
and of themselves as they're a distraction

When I became convinced that I was to seek first the kingdom of God, I tried to give up any plans and ambitions of my own. Most of all, that meant my desire to be a singer and to have a career in the ministry. Since I didn't know whether that was God's will for me and I hadn't received any particular encouragement for a long time, I renounced thoughts of being in music. I wasn't going to think about it anymore. I stopped trying to write songs. And when the normal memories of my former hopes and dreams came to me, I fought them off as temptations. I took my hands off.

One day after taking this position, I was

Chapter 19

DISCERNING GOD'S WILL

*"I was miserable.
Sometimes I would go
home in the middle of
the day just to complain
to Carmel."*

first and all the other things meat and drink represent: status, power, fame. Instead, the kingdom of God is right standing, righteousness, with peace and joy in the Holy Spirit. It's only to be found when our lives are guided by the Spirit. We're not to lean on our own understanding but to acknowledge Him in all our ways so He can direct our paths.

Carmel and I were also participating in a church group at that time in which we were learning how to listen to the prompting of the Spirit—to stay quiet and wait on the Lord for His direction. Of course when you're learning new ways of doing things, from tying your own shoes to shooting a basketball, you do them awkwardly and slowly at first. And sometimes you have to exaggerate the movements to distinguish them from what you're used to.

For example, you have to keep your wrist as stiff as can be when learning to hit a forehand in tennis so you don't swing the racquet like a baseball bat. The Lord seemed to use these techniques of slowing things down and exaggerating the differences in teaching me how to live in a new way.

God had taught me not only about myself through Norman, but also something of Himself. A little boy I know, when I asked him what God says when he prays, replied, "God says yes." Usually, as I was helping Norman, I was preoccupied with how God had *not* granted me what I wanted. But God was saying yes to Norman through me. And He was also saying yes to me through Norman.

The action of God toward us—although we may not understand how—is always the action of love. That's God's nature. He nurtures, encourages, repairs, redeems, forgives, binds up, disciplines (not condemns), transforms, rejoices, creates. Participating in the process of His love toward Norman helped me realize just how God acts toward us and, significantly for me, what I could expect from Him.

I failed Norman many times, most particularly when I read him out in the gangrene episode. But God never makes mistakes like that. He always has all the information. And He always acts on that information in a just, fair, and loving way. I knew God's love for Norman and what that meant in terms of care. And I was overjoyed by the idea that He cared for me in the same way.

My friendship with Norman led me to question my motives, and through this questioning I came to examine my deepest longings and finally my reason for living. I saw that becoming a Christian didn't change me overnight. I had asked God to be my Savior *and* Lord, but at the time I hardly knew all the schemes Mike Adkins had for staying in control. For example, I could take my love of applause and the people-pleasing behavior that went with it and make it into pious do-gooding.

Helping Norman had some positive results, don't get me wrong. It had done him some good, which was the main idea. And it had taught me a lot about my own short-comings.

How, though, was I to change in the ways the experience had taught me I need-ed to change? How was I to act out of grati-tude for God's love and thanksgiving for the creature He had made me to be instead of trying to earn His approval for the person I pretended to be?

When I thought about it, I saw that all my righteousness was as filthy rags, that my good deeds were often a kind of hoax, a way of tricking God into believing in Mike Adkins, the superior being. He knew me. So did I, really. But I liked to pretend I was something better, to lie to myself, and to try to fool God into being a coconspirator. That was sick. But how to be well?

At a church service one night, we sang a chorus based on the passage from Matthew that begins, "Seek ye first the kingdom of God." As I drove home, I kept singing the chorus over and over to myself. Then the thought occurred to me, "What is the king-dom of God?" As I mulled that over, I real-ized I didn't really know the answer. So how was I to seek it if I didn't know what it was?

A short time later, I started doing a Bible study with Carmel, and in that study I found out what the kingdom of God is. It's not meat or drink, the Bible says, though many people in the world seek those things due. That's the way it continued to go until the debt was clear. In fact, God paid off that loan in much less than thirty-six months.

Then I went to a local Christian radio station and asked the folks there to play the album. One of the songs, "Adoration," soon went to number one on their play list. That was exciting, but still I was distrustful. After all, I had lived in the area all my life, and I wondered whether people from other parts of the country would be so positive toward my music.

Another indication that I should become more serious about ministry, however, came through my increasing dissatisfaction with my job. In many ways I had a good job. In a coal-mining community, being an inspector is a respected position, particularly if you're evenhanded in your treatment of labor and management. My father was very proud of me, and since my conversion I had been especially eager to win his approval. I had a good income. As an inspector, too, I wasn't subject to as many risks as the average miner.

Still, I was miserable. Sometimes I would go home in the middle of the day just to complain to Carmel. I hoped, of course, that I wasn't just getting too big for my britches now that I had an album out. I don't think it was that. Someone told me that an experience like this can be like the mother eagle taking the softness out of the nest so that her babies will get up and fly. I think the Lord was doing something like that in urging me to take my ministry seriously. I began to rehearse in my mind how I would resign and what I would say to my boss. I was afraid, though.

Nonetheless, what happened with the album at our local Christian station made a deep impression on me. From this the Lord seemed to say, "Get in your car. Think of it as a tractor. You're going to go out into the fields and plant your seed. These albums are like the farmer's seed. Take them to Christian radio stations, and plant until I tell you you've planted enough. Have your wife, like the farmer's wife, take care of the home and pray for you. Tell her you'll be back when the work is completed." And He impressed one thought on me that I always mention when I speak in churches: "You'll never have a harvest if you don't plant a seed."

The Lord appeared to be calling me clearly to full-time ministry, but I must admit I hedged somewhat in following His guidance. I asked my boss for a leave of absence. I had a two-week vacation coming up, and I was going to use that time for my planting trip. The annual inspectors' picnic at the lake was scheduled at the end of those two weeks, and I would find out then whether my leave of absence had come through.

Chapter
18

GOD'S YES
TO ME

*"When you're learning new
ways of doing things,
. . . you do them awkwardly
and slowly at first. And
sometimes you have to
exaggerate the movements.
. . . The Lord seemed to use
these techniques. . . in
teaching me how to live in
a new way."*

Chapter
20

ON THE ROAD
OF FAITH

*"My father had once
described me as someone
chasing something. When
I gave up the chase, I
found God chasing me
down with just what I
needed again and again."*

Many instances of the Lord's guidance occurred throughout that first promotional/planting trip. Perhaps the most significant came right at the start. I didn't know just how I would find my way from one Christian radio station to another. I looked in the road atlas and mapped out a circuit that would take me through as much territory as possible in the available time, but I didn't know exactly where the stations were located.

Then one day a lady walked up to me at our church and said, "There's another singer who tells me he has a book that tells where all the radio stations in America are. You've got this new album, Mike, and you ought to get that book."

I ignored her advice, because I didn't want to put my hands on the tiller and direct my own course. I just wanted to flow with the Lord.

The day before my trip started, however, this same woman came to our door. "I have a book I want Mike to read," she said. "I just felt like God wanted me to bring it to him."

I must admit I hid from her. I didn't have time, I thought, to read a book. I didn't have time to do anything but get on the road. I was thirty-seven years old and maybe getting black lung disease, so I wasn't about to sit down and read a book that might try to change my theological views the day before I risked all for Jesus. (I had forgotten the nature of the book.) But I knew both the woman and my wife would pin me down later and ask whether I had looked at the book, so I came out of hiding and accepted it.

It turned out to be the National Religious Broadcasters' annual directory, which includes the address of every member radio station in the nation. The woman who brought it to me kept saying that she had felt God wanted me to have it, and that from the "polite" way I had responded to her when she made the suggestion, she wasn't sure I would order it. So she had ordered it herself and had come to give it to me.

With that book in hand, I was able to hit

about every Christian radio station in a three-state area.

My father had once described me as someone chasing something. Once I gave up the chase, I found God chasing me down with just what I needed—like that book—again and again.

God gave me two directions in my dealings with the radio stations. As mentioned earlier, He had impressed upon me the idea that I shouldn't hype my album. He would be a better salesman than I could ever be. And He also impressed upon me the importance of always being polite.

With those guidelines fixed in mind, I went into those stations and said, "I'm Mike Adkins. I'm from Illinois, and I'm a coal miner. I'd like to leave this with you for your consideration." That's all I would say. Then I'd leave quickly unless they stopped me.

One day I went into an old bank building in Joplin, Missouri, where there was supposed to be a station. A Christian bookstore had purchased the building, and it was huge—as big as the city hall in our town. There was only one customer in the bookstore, and a young woman was behind the cash register. She directed me to the station on the second floor.

On the way up in the elevator, I got an overwhelming feeling that the Lord would have me give that young woman ten dollars.

I thought, "I'm not sure I've got enough money to make this trip, even with staying at cheap motels, watching my gasoline, and eating nothing but moon pies and Dr. Pepper!" But then I thought, "Hey, I'm out here on a limb for the Lord already. I've got to go for it."

So when I came back down, I walked over to her and said, "Sweetheart, are you troubled about something?"

"Yes, sir," she said, and she got big tears in her eyes.

"Is it financial?"

She nodded. I knew I was a dead duck. I gave her the ten dollars, and she said, "That's exactly what I have to have today, the very amount."

I was pleased I had been able to help. I didn't think much more about it but just went on my way.

Shortly after leaving Joplin you get into Oklahoma, and one of the first towns across the border is Miami. I needed gas, so I pulled off there. While I pumped, I looked around and noticed a beautiful, new church up the road.

The Lord seemed to say to me, "Go over there."

"God, I don't have time to visit churches," I prayed. "I'm not trying to sing in churches. I'm trying to visit as many radio stations as I can in a very limited time. I may not be able to get to enough stations as it is to get a true reading on people's response. If I'm seriously thinking about not only taking a leave of absence but even quitting my job one day, I've got to know for sure. . . ."

I went on arguing with God like that for a while. Finally, I drove over and visited with the pastor, Gerald Baser, a nice, quiet man. He listened to my whole album right there in his study. He leaned back in his chair and didn't say a single word. I sat there feeling stupid and thinking, "I'm bothering this man. I sure hope my old Pontiac starts when I get out to it again."

When the last song ended, I got up and said, "Brother Baser, I appreciate your time." He didn't say anything, and I left feeling dumber than ever.

As I opened the car door, however, he came rushing out of the church, saying, "Wait a minute! Wait a minute! Don't leave. I was trying to listen to God. I believe the Lord wants you to come back here tomorrow night and do our entire church service."

I said that I'd like to but didn't know how I could, because that would put me too far behind in my schedule.

"Let me be honest with you," he said. "I've had a number of guests in here lately, speakers and singers, and I shouldn't have another one for a while. I've got to speak to my own people. But I know the Lord wants you to do the service tomorrow night."

"Do you have a motel in this town?" I asked.

He said yes.

"Is it clean and inexpensive?"

He said it was fine.

"If I go there right now and make myself go to bed and get to sleep, which is the hardest thing in the world for me to do—I'm always so keyed up after driving—and put my clothes out and get up in the morning and jump in them before dawn and get on down to Tulsa earlier than I had first planned, then I could drive back here in the afternoon and be in time for the evening service."

That's what we agreed I would do.

When I went to the motel, I got my key and pulled around to the room. Parked right next to me was a beautiful, blue Cadillac with a diesel engine—very popular in those days. I stood there and admired it. It was gorgeous. My dad thought that if you owned a Cadillac, you were John D. Rockefeller. Just then, the people who owned it came out of their room, and I told them how much I admired their car.

"You have an eight-track player, I'll bet," I said. They did, so I continued, "Let me give you a tape. It's free. I just want you to have it."

They invited me to dinner, but I made my apologies, as I was determined to go straight to bed.

I went in and took a shower in order to relax and get sleepy. There I was, singing in the shower, feeling great, when the thought struck me—and again I felt it was from the Lord—"Those folks are going to give me something." Then my mind leaped ahead and I thought, "They're going to give me that Cadillac." I could see me driving it home. I would leave my old Pontiac right where it was parked and never give it another thought.

The next morning I woke up early, got dressed, and went out to my car. "It's time, Lord," I said to Him. "If they're going to give me something, now's the time." Nobody was around, and nobody was going to *come* around. This was still before dawn. I started thinking, "Am I getting crazy? Am I becoming a fanatic? Who wants to be a fanatic?"

I realized I was going to have to leave, so I opened my front door. And there on the seat—they had slipped it between the rubber-sealed windows—was a ten-dollar bill.

As I drove out of Miami into Tulsa, God seemed to say to me, "You remember the ten dollars I had you give away yesterday? I wanted to show you I can take care of you if I send you out here." That was the moment when I first thought, really and truly, that He might want me and my family in full-time ministry.

That night, five minutes before the service started, Brother Baser's wife came up to me. "I didn't understand why my husband invited you," she said. "We've had a lot of guests lately, but he was so sure God was in it. Now I know why." She explained that in the last hour he had called his mother, who lived in California. She had been sick for a long time. And when he called, he received the news that she had passed away. The pastor's wife said, "My husband's in no shape to do this meeting tonight, and I believe God sent you here because tonight my husband needs a minister."

That night I sang "Be at Peace My Child," a song I wrote the night Elvis Presley died:

Be at peace My child,
I am aware of you.
Though trouble may seem
to be too much to bear,
be at peace My child.

When I wrote the song, I felt that God was speaking to me personally. I had been so troubled about not having any success in the music business, and I was grieving for the loss of Elvis, which in some way symbolized the loss of my own hopes as well. The Lord had given me the song to comfort me. It hasn't been one of my "hits," but it has ministered to desperately hurting people. Folks walk up to me in meetings all the time and say, "You know that song on your album, 'Be at Peace My Child'? My husband died of cancer, and that's the only way I made it. I played that thing until I wore it out."

After I sang the song that night, the whole congregation gathered around their pastor, prayed for him, and sent him off to California for his mother's funeral. He knew they loved him and would be praying for him. And that night I had further confirmation that God had a place for us in the ministry.

At the last radio station on my planting trip, the deejay not only played my album, but he also interviewed me on the spot, which was a great boost. When I got in the car to head for home, I switched on the station, and my song was playing again. That encouraged me like nobody's business.

At the inspectors' annual picnic, my boss and I took a walk together through a stand of cottonwood trees, the fluff blowing through the air and covering the grass like a child's downy blanket. He cleared his throat and said, "We couldn't get you a leave of absence. I approved it, and the district manager approved it, but when it got to D.C., they called back and scolded us. Their attitude is, 'You guys are cooperating with this man, and he's just wanting to change jobs. What's the matter with you!' I'm sorry,

Mike, but they turned it down."

"Well, you tried," I said.

"We did try. We like your work. And I guess *you'll* have to like it a while longer. We'll see you back at work on Monday."

"No, sir," I said, then swallowed. "I'm going to resign."

He looked at me and answered, "I thought you were going to say that." We both lowered our eyes and walked on a few paces. "Can you come in Monday morning and turn in your equipment?"

I did, although I didn't want to. I wanted to get back on the road. But the Lord seemed to say it would be loving if I did. And it proved to be a good thing for me, because my boss corrected a misimpression I had about having to forfeit my retirement money. I had been there not quite ten years, and I thought you had to be there the full ten to draw on your retirement savings. I ended up collecting $11,600. From that we got down to $100 in the bank so fast you couldn't believe it, but we did have a little breathing space as we began our full-time ministry in the summer of 1979.

My faith through all these things came out of my involvement with Norman. Without our friendship, I would never have trusted enough in God as a caring, loving Father who wants us to have the desires of our hearts if we'll put Him first.

Chapter 21

EVIDENCE OF BLESSING

"When we heard the mailman's step on the porch and the mail drop into the aluminum box, we tried to act as if we weren't expecting anything special, but of course we were."

I went back on the road for a while after that, visiting more radio stations and finishing with the weekend singing invitations I had already started to accept. In the next few weeks, I would be waiting for the results of my planting trips.

I had heard that some great Christian leaders of the past, people like George Mueller, had found money in their mailboxes just when they needed it—many times from anonymous sources. I talked about this with Carmel and our girls on the way home from my last known singing engagement, and, since we were truly relying on the Lord now for our income, we waited to see if He would do the same kind of thing for us.

We passed through the living room often that day, trying to spy the mailman coming up the walk. When we heard his step on the porch and the mail drop into the aluminum box, we tried to act as if we weren't expecting anything special, but of course we were. I opened the door as casually as I could, retrieved our mail, and looked through it.

A check for five dollars came that day. Someone had heard one of my songs and ordered a copy, and I had sent it out earlier. We knew the source of the funds and why they had been sent, but that check still seemed like a miracle to us. (We handled all the distribution of that first album out of our home.) On Tuesday there was another check for five dollars, on Wednesday another, and on Thursday there was a check for thirty dollars from a Christian bookstore to which I had mailed several albums on consignment.

I went over to my dad's and showed him the checks. I wanted him to see what God was doing for us. He was extremely skeptical about my course of action. To tell the truth, it deeply grieved him that I had resigned from my inspector's job. He thought the checks that had come in were fine, but he reminded me I had a lot of years ahead of me in which to support my family. "I know there's a God," he said, "and your mom has always been religious, but I'm not sure I can agree with what you're doing now."

All I could tell him was that I was doing, as best I could, what the Lord was telling me to do. I desperately hoped I was doing the right thing and hadn't misheard the Lord this time. My father made me doubt myself. He had practical, good sense on his side, after all. And I had always prospered following his advice; rarely when I ran against it. I kept reminding myself that I also had a heavenly Father, however, and that it was my obligation to obey Him first. But I listened to my dad. I *listened*.

I had been invited to sing that weekend in Lafayette, Indiana, to a ladies' Bible study group. My sister and brother-in-law who live in the area attended as well. We wanted to fit in a visit together.

After the service, one of the few men in attendance came up to talk to me. I had never seen him before. He looked like any other gentleman, perfectly normal, except that I could see he had been upset or moved in some way. His hands were shaking.

"God spoke to me during this meeting," he said, "and I've never had that happen before." He asked if I believed in the principle of planting seeds in order to have a harvest.

That shocked me, since that principle had become the very foundation of my ministry. I said I certainly did believe in it.

"Well," he said, "I'm going to plant some

seed. The Lord told me to give you an offering. How much should I give you?"

The Lord had counseled me never to beg for money, so I replied in the way I thought I should. "Sir, I'm trying to have integrity," I told him, "and if I were you, I wouldn't give me a dime if you aren't sure that God told you to give me this gift. I don't want you giving just because your emotions may have been stirred up."

As much as I could have used a large offering, I felt I had done the right thing.

The man took his wife by the hand and left. Then I wasn't so sure I had said what I should have! In fact, I felt like hitting my head on the pulpit.

After a few minutes, however, when most of the group had gone, he and his wife came back in and stopped me in the church aisle. "Listen," he said, "we went out in the car and prayed, and God told us to give you something." He looked up at his wife, who was taller, and asked, "Honey, how much should we give him?"

"What did the Lord tell you to give him during the meeting?" she answered. "That's what you do, exactly."

No more was said. He sat down and wrote me a check for four thousand dollars!

Carmel was standing right beside me. She thanked them profusely and told them we would be praying for them. I was absolutely in shock. I'm not even sure I was polite about it. I mean, I ran red lights on the way home!

I hadn't told anyone publicly about this, but I had continued to write songs, and that next week I planned to go back to the recording studio and do another album. But God had impressed upon me that I should trust Him completely for my finances this time. I could have gone back to the bank, but I was sure God wanted me to let Him do it alone this time. Of course I had no idea how He planned to accomplish this until that husband and wife handed me their check.

My father went with me to the recording sessions. He liked singing as much as I did—maybe more. He especially liked to lead people in singing at family Christmas gatherings. The studio sessions lasted for hours. Dad eventually got tired and went back to the motel before we finished.

When I came in late that night, he was already in bed, although not yet asleep. I got ready myself, slipped under the covers, and turned out the light.

I lay there in the darkness for a few minutes, but neither of us could get to sleep. Then he asked me, "Son, how much did all that cost today? Them violins and singers and guitars and everything that's going to be on the record."

"The bill is over there, Dad." It came to $3,995.

After he got up and took a look, he said, "Son, do you realize how close that is to the four thousand dollars that fellow gave you?"

I could tell Dad found the coincidence astonishing. The Holy Spirit was speaking to him in a deeper way than ever before. I wept quietly there in the darkness, because I knew he had been touched.

Two weeks later, my mom called home from a vacation trip to Florida. She was so excited as she said, "After praying and witnessing to your father for forty years, I saw him go forward in a church service last night and give his heart to Jesus!"

My father's conversion changed him so much I could hardly believe it. He had always been a good man in a natural way. But he was a big man and a tough one, and he came from the old school when it came to discipline, both at home and on the job. If a fellow at the mine wasn't working as hard as my dad thought he should be, he wasn't shy about confronting him. Now he became gentleness itself.

Chapter 22

DAD'S HOMEGOING

"Through Norman I started living the life of faith in earnest, and my father saw what faith can do."

Two years after his conversion, my father was diagnosed as having pancreatic cancer. The doctors gave him six months to live, and he lived for exactly six more months.

I went to see him the day before he died. Looking at him in the bed, I didn't know whether he would recognize me or not. I asked him, "Dad, do you know me?"

He looked at me real strange and said, "Well, I reckon you're still Mike, aren't ya?"

When I got control of my emotions again, I said, "I know I broke your heart, Dad, when I was a teenager. When I was touring, I never called home. I didn't write. I know you were worried about me, and I'm sorry."

"That's OK, Son," he said, "we turned out to be pretty good buddies after all."

Pretty good buddies. How much that meant to me!

I went home for the day, but the next morning I woke up at six o'clock and felt an urgency from God to dress quickly and go to the hospital. My eight brothers and sisters had visited Dad many times during those six months of illness, but I hadn't seen him as much as I would have liked. I treasured every moment now.

My brother-in-law Luke sat by his bedside when I entered the room that morning. "He's really weak, Mike," Luke said. "I don't think he can hear us." Luke had stayed up with him most of the night.

"Go on home and rest, Luke, if you want," I said. "I'll sit with him."

Luke told me the nurse was going to check Dad's blood pressure in a few minutes, and with that, he left and went home.

I watched Dad for a while. In a few minutes, I wasn't sure he was breathing. I went up close to make sure I was seeing right. He'd go for a long moment and wouldn't breathe, and then he'd breathe again.

At that point I felt led by the Spirit to take the comb the hospital had provided and comb Dad's hair for him. My dad wouldn't go anywhere unless he had his hair combed. And I knew then—and a peace came over me—that the Lord was going to take him home.

So I combed his white hair. I combed it down, parted it, and styled it right. Once again I was struck by the closeness in age between Norman and Dad. And I thought how my experience with Norman had paved the way for so much, including rec- onciliation with my father. Through Norman I started living the life of faith in earnest, and my father had seen what faith can do.

Dad was about to die, but he would die unafraid. I knew God had helped him undo his own life of fear—fear of not being able to put bread on the table, of the mines and what could happen any day, at any moment. I felt we had conquered the fear together. He could die now because he was combed, washed, and ready for the new company he was about to join. Unafraid.

His breathing became slower and slower. I don't know how to describe it except to say that his breathing was like the engine on a lawn mower, and someone was steadily turning down the accelerator, the engine running more and more slowly. Finally it cut off, and he was gone.

I miss my dad—how I miss him! But we had gotten to be pretty good buddies after all, friends at last after a lifetime of struggle, each confident in the other's love.

Chapter 23

MY FRIEND,
THE TV STAR

*"It dawned on me that
probably no one had kissed
and hugged Norman since
his mother died some ten
years before. What a lonely
life he had lived!"*

After the albums came out, I started appearing on Christian television in 1980. And one of the program directors at a national network asked me whether I didn't tell a story about a Herman or something. (I had begun to talk about my experience with Norman. I'll tell why directly.)

"Yes, sure, you mean Norman," I said.

She asked me if I'd like to bring him on the daily program and sing a song I wrote about him.

That sounded like a good idea to me, and I promised her I would ask Norman about it.

Norman wanted to go. In fact, he was enthusiastic about it. So we drove to the St.

Louis airport and caught a jumbo jet. As we started down the runway, I looked over at Norman and said, "Norman, you've just been a Christian a short time, and God's already blessing you like this."

He looked at me and said, "I've been marvelously blessed."

Then he repeated, "I've been marvelously blessed."

On the way down, Norman spent almost all his time looking out the window. I had made sure he got a window seat, which I knew he would like. At one point he said, "Those must be the Smoky Mountains down there."

He was right. Shyness sometimes causes Norman to have trouble expressing himself, and he withdraws in personal encounters with unfamiliar people, but he isn't retarded. He's an intelligent man who struggles in dealing with the outside world. It's always a mistake to think him mentally slow. In fact, he managed to graduate from high school. He must have remembered the Smoky Mountains from a grade-school geography lesson.

When we arrived, I checked us into a motel, and then we went to the station. They put makeup on us. Norman got a big kick out of that. Everyone was very cordial to him, making a fuss over him. He was a celebrity!

Before the broadcast started, the program director came to me and said we would have only eight minutes for our segment, so I didn't get to tell the Norman story that day. I just sang the song to him that I had written about the experience. And then a local businessman, Bill Williams, came out and presented Norman with a brand-new, power lawn mower. Old Grasscutter never looked happier.

Next the host's wife came over and kissed Norman on the cheek, and that pleased him no end.

After eating lunch with the cast and crew, we went back to the motel room. That night, we were able to watch a rebroadcast of the morning's program. Norman saw the host's wife kiss him again. He threw his head back, grinned, and chuckled to himself. "I think she likes me," he said.

"I'm sure she does, Norman," I said. "She already has a husband, though."

He looked at me as if I were the afflicted one. "I didn't mean anything like that," he said.

Then it dawned on me that probably no one had kissed and hugged Norman since his mother died some ten years before. What a lonely life he had lived! What a tragedy that so many people like Norman live without any kind of emotional support! They never have anyone embrace them and tell them how much they're loved. I wondered that night whether I would be capable of living such a life.

Norman's experiences with other people had been almost entirely negative. No wonder he had roared at me like the Incredible Hulk so long ago! He must have felt he needed to make people afraid of him at times in order to not be victimized by them. I thought of the way Christ had turned and ministered to the lepers when others wouldn't even let them approach. He had healed them with His touch, while we so often make people into social lepers by turning away.

NORMAN'S LIFE TODAY

"In the best sense, Norman is childlike — a child with the heart of a lion."

For the last few years, Norman has lived at the American Beauty Nursing Home in West Frankfort. Since his leg needs constant professional care and he has gotten on in years, Norman decided it would be best for him to move there.

The nursing home serves its residents well. Norman gets three balanced meals a day now—more hot food than he's had in a lifetime. He's gained twenty pounds that look good on him. His leg is cleaned and bandaged regularly, and he can't get a cold without a doctor's having a look at him. The home provides activities as well. Norman has been back to see the Cardinals play baseball a half dozen times. And he recently won second place in the basketball free-throw event at a nursing home special Olympics and had his picture put in the newspaper. The home also has people come in to entertain, and it gathers the residents together for socials.

Still, many of the residents are infirm and often bedfast. When I go to visit Norman, the place strikes me as a small world. It's very much like the world outside: most of its residents are unhappy. In the larger world, more people have their physical health, but they have spiritual ailments that make them just as miserable.

For Norman, however, it's been a good situation. I wish you could see how success-fully he has adapted, how at peace he is living in the nursing home. From the apathetic stares of some of his fellow residents, they seem to have resigned themselves to dying. They act as if the nursing home must be the gateway into a dismal eternity. But that's not true of Norman at all. He lives a full life there.

Norman shares a room with three other men. His personal space is neat and tidy. The bed is made. Norman gets up every morning, washes (yes, he does now!), and dresses for the day. He keeps all his clothing and personal articles in his storage locker just like a well-disciplined soldier. He always has something to read in his "library section," usually an article or a book on how God has moved in an individual's life. You have a sense there in his room that Norman knows how to "abide and abound," to accept whatever life presents with gratitude and make the best of it.

Since becoming a Christian, Norman has gone through a normal spiritual growth process. God has been working to conform him to the image of Christ, and, as with all of us, that's meant more struggle in some areas than in others. In Norman's case, one of the things he felt led to do was to quit smoking cigarettes, and that was a real battle. But with God's help, he eventually won and broke the habit.

Norman has also seen the movie that's been made about our friendship and how it developed, and he got many a chuckle out of it. Afterward, he commented on how well it showed the way people in town had mis-understood him all those years. And then he said something that I think shows just how much he's grown up spiritually. "You know, Mike," he told me, "the message and what I believe God wants to do with this film are what's most important about it."

Norman takes a daily walk, usually in the morning. He visits his old house across the street from mine almost every day. For the first time he has friends his own age, and he likes to socialize with them in the day room. People around town speak to him more normally now, and he's seeing himself as more normal. He's also getting letters from people across the country who've heard his story.

He becomes fascinated with one game or another for several weeks at a time. Recently, he and a friend were devoted to a racing game in which they steered their markers around a track toward the imaginary finish line. Norman makes friends easily. And when he loses friends, through death or their moving away, he grieves but doesn't become bitter. Instead, he takes the risk of loving and befriends the next person.

I wish I could convey all that Norman has taught me about how to live. In the beginning, thinking so much of what I wanted to teach him, I hardly considered the possibility that he might have a great deal to teach me. But Norman renewed my sense of wonder in the world. He taught me to be more trusting. I think of how often Norman has been the victim of others, and yet he was willing to take the chance that I might actually want to be his friend.

Most of all, I think, Norman showed me how to take life as it comes. I tend to carry my feelings from the past into the present, to experience a friendship or an event as another instance of something I already know about. By doing so, I sometimes blind myself to what's fresh and new in the experience.

But Norman looks at things for just what they are. If people mistreat him, they mistreat him. The next person may befriend him, and he remains entirely open to that possibility. When you think about it, much of our normal way of looking at life has to do with turning our fears, resentments, and self-regard into "good reasons" for avoiding much of what really makes life worthwhile. Norman simply doesn't do this. In the best sense, he's childlike—a child with the heart of a lion, for Norman has endured much of what most of us fear so terribly. The Lord said, "A little child shall lead them" (Isa. 11:6), and Norman has led me into understanding why.

THANK YOU, LORD, FOR NORMAN

"When I accepted Norman, I also accepted the hurting part of myself."

The success of my first album took me back to Ridgecrest campgrounds. I was there to do the music while a speaker brought the messages. But the speaker became ill one night, unfortunately, and the people in charge asked me to fill in for him.

I wasn't sure what I would speak on. I had been studying Isaiah 58, however, and had been struck by these verses: "Is not this the fast that I have chosen? to loose the bands of wickedness, . . . to deal thy bread to the hungry, and that thou bring the poor that are cast out to thy house? when thou seest the naked, that thou cover him; and that thou hide not thyself from thine own flesh?" (verses 6-7).

I couldn't understand that last line from my King James Bible. How can we turn away from our own flesh? I looked up the verse in another translation and saw that it meant our own flesh and blood, our kin, our family.

But I also saw that my mistake might have taught me something, for we, in our own flesh, are the poor. We all need to be nurtured, to be raised up, to be consoled in the grieving that's an inevitable part of life. When we turn away from those who have less than we do, who are less gifted, who are not within our social circle, we're actually turning away from ourselves, because we're denying we have the same needs they have for food and shelter, for love and forgiveness. When we deny that, we make it impossible for God and others to nurture us, and we become poor indeed. To turn away like this is to commit a kind of suicide—to hide from our own humanity.

When I wanted to keep the Normans of the world out of my life, I was caught up in my own illusions of greatness, the lie I wanted to tell myself, the lie I wanted everyone around me to agree in by praising me. So when I accepted Norman, I also accepted the hurting part of myself.

I saw myself out by that tree stump that first day when we had our memorable encounter. I then had about as much understanding of what it took to love my neighbor as myself as I did of what it would take to uproot that stump. I didn't understand how far the roots of pride went down. I didn't know what actions I would have to undertake to come to terms with all of this. I thought I was going to get after it with the trowel of a few kind words, a little hand tool to clear the field of my soul. I needed the engine of God's mysterious action in my life to uproot my vanity and ambition and materialism—to allow the seed of His Word to mature into the finest wheat of His presence.

God *had* worked with me through my friendship with Norman, though. Looking back on the experience, I could see how much I had changed. Relinquishing my hopes for my singing career seemed crucial. I needed to put God first, even to the point of excluding everything else (the only way I was capable of putting God first). That was the day, I think, that the metal chains of God's hold on me grew taut and hauled out that tree stump of pride.

I needed to see as well that God's blocking of my career had been part of His mercy toward me, that He truly wanted the best for me. We have to lose our lives in God to be saved by Him.

Because of my father's insistence on self-reliance and the way he had instilled that in me as a virtue, giving my dreams over to God had been particularly difficult. I had to undertake the role of extending mercy to Norman, in my own halfhearted way, in order to believe at a deep level that God always acts toward us in the same fashion.

When I combed my father's hair just before his death, I realized that I had helped prepare us both for death—the death of pride as well as physical death—by reaching out to Norman. Instead of self-reliance as self-sufficiency, we both came to understand it as responsibility. For we are to acknowledge God in our ways—do the right thing—letting Him direct our paths. We have to be modest in our claims about what we can control in our lives in order to let God be sovereign. Otherwise we end up pretending to ourselves that we can control our own destinies. (If God's not in control, it seems as though someone ought to be, and usually we place ourselves in that position.)

Because I had stopped playing God in my life, I had helped my father do the same in his, and together we had seen God be God. In the events of my early ministry, we had seen God demonstrate His ability to transform the world from a place in which little can be expected to one in which all things are possible.

I read on in Isaiah 58:

Then shall thy light break forth as the morning, and thine health shall spring forth speedily: and thy righteousness shall go before thee; the glory of the LORD shall be thy rereward.

Then shalt thou call, and the LORD shall answer; thou shalt cry, and he shall say, Here I am. . . . And the LORD shall guide thee continually, and satisfy thy soul in drought, and make fat thy bones: and thou shalt be like a watered garden, and like a spring of water, whose waters fail not.

And they that shall be of thee shall build the old waste places: thou shalt raise up the foundations of many generations; and thou shalt be called, The repairer of the breach, The restorer of paths to dwell in. (verses 8, 9, 11-12)

I felt that these promises had been borne out in my life, not so much because God was giving me success in what I wanted to do but because I knew a spiritual health I had never known before. The glory in my life was the Lord's glory. He was my guide. He tended the garden of my soul. He supervised the repairs in my life and restored misguided intentions to their proper ends. Whether my ministry ended or continued, I knew that God would always be working in me. Finally what mattered was holiness and nothing else—being right with God.

As I read those verses again and thought these things through, I sensed the Lord was saying to me, "You can tell it now. Go ahead and tell people about Norman tonight."

I wanted to be sure that was what He was saying, so I argued with God in my prayer, concluding, "I don't want to trade on what You've done."

"It's not a story about you anymore," God seemed to say. "It's My story. You go on and tell it. I want people to know that I'll do for anyone what I did for you. I'll give them life."

So I got up that night at Ridgecrest and told the story of a man called Norman.

DON'T MISS
THE FILM!

The compelling, true story of *A Man Called Norman*, featuring Mike Adkins, is now available on film and videotape. A gifted speaker and evangelist, Mike appeals to all ages as he drives home one of the most profound commandments in the Bible—to love your neighbor as yourself.

Produced by Focus on the Family Films, this resource is ideal for evening church services, youth groups, and Sunday school classes. Don't miss this dynamic presentation from the producers of *Twice Pardoned*.

The film's popular theme song, "Proud to Be Your Friend," is available on the record album *Focus* by Chris Christian, from Home Sweet Home Records, and can be purchased at your local Christian bookstore.

Other Faith and Family Strengtheners
From Focus on the Family®

Molder of Dreams
Encouragement is a powerful force, and one that lasts. In this compelling account, 1986 Teacher of the Year Guy Doud shares a moving message on the profound difference affirmation and love will have in the lives of others . . .*when we're willing to invest the time.* Paperback. *Also available in video.*

Great Stories Remembered and Great Stories Remembered II
Families love these forgotten collections of touching accounts, warm narrations and exciting adventures dating back to the turn of the century. Each classic tale highlights timeless virtues and inspiring morals. Great gift books! Hardcover. *Also available in audiocassette.*

• • •

9BPXCL

FOCUS ON THE FAMILY®
Welcome to the Family!

Whether you received this book as a gift, borrowed it from
a friend, or purchased it yourself, we're glad you read it!
It's just one of the many helpful, insightful, and encouraging
resources produced by Focus on the Family.

In fact, that's what Focus on the Family is all about—
providing inspiration, information, and biblically based
advice to people in all stages of life.

It began in 1977 with the vision of one man, Dr. James Dobson,
a licensed psychologist and author of 16 best-selling books on
marriage, parenting, and family. Alarmed by the societal, political,
and economic pressures that were threatening the existence
of the American family, Dr. Dobson founded Focus on the Family
with one employee—an assistant—and a once-a-week
radio broadcast aired on only 36 stations.

Now an international organization, Focus on the Family is
dedicated to preserving Judeo-Christian values and strengthening
the family through more than 70 different ministries, including
eight separate daily radio broadcasts; television public service
announcements; 11 publications; and a steady series of
award-winning books, films, and videos for people
of all ages and interests.

Recognizing the needs of, as well as the sacrifices and important
contribution made by, such diverse groups as educators, physi-
cians, attorneys, crisis pregnancy center staff, and single parents,
Focus on the Family offers specific outreaches to uphold and minister to these individuals, too. And it's all done for one purpose
and one purpose only: to encourage and strengthen individuals
and families through the life-changing message of Jesus Christ.

• • •

For more information about the ministry, or if we can be of help to
your family, simply write to Focus on the Family, Colorado Springs,
CO 80995 or call 1-800-A-FAMILY (1-800-232-6459). Friends in
Canada may write Focus on the Family, P.O. Box 9800, Stn.
Terminal, Vancouver, B.C. V6B 4G3 or call 1-800-661-9800. Visit our
Web site—www.family.org—to learn more about the ministry or to
find out if there is a Focus on the Family office in your country.

We'd love to hear from you!

THAT'S WEIRD NORMAN!

"My immediate response
to seeing Norman come
around that corner was to
feel betrayed by God."

Chapter

1

WEST FRANKFORT,
ILLINOIS

*"As in all small towns,
where everybody knows most
everybody else, people in
West Frankfort still care
what others think of them."*

Chapter
6

WHO'S THE
WEIRD ONE?

*"No one in town knew
what was wrong with
Norman, not really."*

Chapter
9

TAKE ME OUT TO THE BALL GAME

"Before the end of the third inning I had bought Norman soft drinks, peanuts, popcorn, nacho cheese chips, and ice cream—practically everything they sold at the ball park except beer."

(left) In a dramatic scene from the film version of the story, these kids put a bucket of water over Norman's door on Halloween night, symbolizing the indignities he suffered in years past.

(below) In the same scene from the movie, the "monster" many people thought Norman might be comes after the boys who tried to douse him.

Mike tells the story of his friendship with Norman before a live audience during the making of the film.

That winter, I went for a week's training at a school for mine inspectors in West Virginia. And toward the end of the week, I received an emergency call that pulled me out of class. "Mike, it's Norman," Carmel said. "He fell, and they say he's done a lot of damage to his knee."

"Where is he now?" I asked.

"You really need to get home as soon as you can."

"OK," I said, "but where is he now?"

"They're taking him to the hospital. It's not life and death, but he's asking for you."

I hurried home as soon as I could and went directly to the hospital. Norman was lying in bed. I noticed how clean he looked:

I hadn't been able to get him to keep bathing, and he'd undergone another transformation at the nurses' hands.

The doctor came in and told me that Norman had dislocated his knee severely, tearing the ligaments and chipping the bone as well. I found out Norman had fallen a total of three times—the first time downtown, and then twice while trying to get home. Once a knee destabilizes, it will go out easily again, and Norman's feet had been sliding around on the icy sidewalks as he made his painful way home. He must have increased the damage with each fall.

Norman stayed in the hospital for several weeks, hooked up to IVs as the staff stabilized the knee and tried to reduce the swelling. The doctor pointed out that Norman would be bedfast for a time after he went home and that he would need someone to care for him. He would also need someone to help him carry on a program of physical therapy, exercising the knee so it wouldn't remain stiff and limit his mobility permanently.

When he went home, the Meals on Wheels people came. For the rest, I took care of him.

When I went over in the evenings, I would run the bath and help him get into it so that he could soak the leg. Then I would help him back to the bed. There, while he

Chapter
15

QUIET COURAGE

*"Norman came out of his
bedroom and into the
hall.... Suddenly, I saw his
leg. It was swollen almost
double its normal size!"*